Fragments of Addiction

By Robert

& Paris

Bauldwin

ISBN 978-0-615-44738-4
90000

9 780615 447384

PROLOGUE

Fragments-smaller pieces of something whole, usually unidentifiable in their shattered state, but once pieced together, fragments can create a remarkably, breathtaking masterpiece.

Most of our lives can be told in fragments: fragments of sacrifice, fragments of turmoil, fragments of tragedy, and fragments of joy. Each of these fragments, augmenting together to form something complete and wonderful; much like the beautiful tiles of a mosaic.

On a recent visit to Rome, I was so overwhelmed by the breathtaking splendor of the cobblestone streets in Piazza Navona. Amongst the amazing fountains and decadent shops, were little pieces of history that most people commonly disregard, as their feet walk over them to their choice museum or restaurant. The cobblestone, and not the magnificent marble sculptures that resided in the center of the beautiful fountains and talented street performers, held my attention, as I thought about how long the cobblestone had been there.

I imagined all the things that the cobblestone had endured: torrential rain, adverse temperatures, and frenzied debates at the base of the Pasquino. I thought about the many people from the corners of the Earth who had traversed the cobblestone with no thought for the history they were walking over, the beauty that they were converging with. Looking at an individual cobblestone is like staring at a rock; it may have aged gum on it, and smell like whiskey from a spilt drink the night before, however, looking at them all together, was looking at the past and relishing in true beauty. Each fragment, each cobblestone setting the atmosphere for one of the most beautiful places I have ever seen with my own eyes.

This book will piece together the many cobblestones of the lives of people, much like myself, that have lived with addiction, whether it was there own or someone else's. These cobblestones, these fragments, separate, tell the stories of much heartache and tribulation, however, once pieced together, show a brilliant trend of resilience, perseverance, beauty and hope.

Addiction plagues more people than the average person commonly acknowledges. I know growing up, I thought that my family was unique in that several of my family members, immediate and extended, suffered from drug addiction, leaving fragments of solitude behind to us, their children who had to suffer in silence. However, the sad truth about addiction is it is far too common and my story is one of millions, creating many fragments of addiction.

You are not alone in your journey to recovery. You are not alone.

Paris Bauldwin

FORWARD

Hi my name is Robert Bauldwin and I am an addict. I was blessed to wake up next to my wife, my beautiful wife Jean, who I love more than any woman I have ever met in my life. Jean, you are beautiful and haven given breath to my collapsing lungs. I thank God for bringing you to me.

To my beautiful, three boys, Robert, Justin and Bryson, I love you all so very much. You have given me the opportunity to be a better father...a more present father and I love you all so very much. You all are destined to be great, and I am so proud of you all. Stay in school, and remember to always finish what you start. With God all things are possible, and even when I am not there cheering you on, know that I am always with you. You can do all things that you put your mind to.

I was blessed to be able to talk with Paris, and have her share her happiness with me. I am so proud of you, Paris. Your father, here on earth, and your Father up in heaven, commend the woman that you have become. We love you so much. Continue your walk with God. Continue on the beaten path to happiness and success. The sky is the limit and I can't wait to see all of your dreams come true, because I know with great certainty that they will.

Roberta, my precious, fragile daughter, you remind me of my mother Roberta. You are my hero. These last few years have given me so much joy, so it is okay to be sappy and sentimental. Thank you for my father's day card. As I wipe tears out of my eyes, I want you to know how much I love you and admire your strength. You are remarkable and I am so thankful for your vigor and perseverance. There are not many people in the world that have your strength and sensibility. You make me overwhelmingly proud.

Chris, I love you with all of my heart. I know I haven't been the best father to you, but I want you to know it isn't because of you. I just never knew how to be a father to a little boy, but believe that I love you so much that it hurts. It hurts me so much more that I couldn't have been a better father to you. You are so dear to my heart, and I want you to know that I have always loved you and I always will. I admire the man you were able to become, even in my absence, and I know that you will be a better father than I was to you. You are an incredible man.

Tiffany Fantasia, I love you. You were my first love, my first beautiful girl. Fantasia means a free composition structured according to the composer's fancy...God is such an amazing composer, isn't he? You have a critical sensibility for a romantic attachment, but all you need is God. He loves you more than ANYONE or ANYTHING in this galaxy or the next. Let Him love you how I could not.

I remember when you walked into the house and you saw me drinking a beer. You knew right away that I had betrayed you and the piercing look in your eyes ate at my soul. I know it shattered your heart and I want to ask you for forgiveness. Forgive me for all of the wrong I have ever done to you. I did not finish my fatherhood, and I am so sorry to all of you for that, but allow God to pick up from where I left off. He loves you. I love you. That's all.

Shame & Hope

Low, low, lower than the ground, but higher than the heavens. I've given myself away to a stranger, not one…. seven… and it's only Tuesday- I pray that this ground will break away, so I can go where I belong. I pray this ground gives way, so I can be where I feel; where I fell. Low, low, lower than the ground, but higher than the heavens.

HELLO, MY NAME IS ROBERT BAULDWIN, AND I AM AN ADDICT.... I have one day today and a lot of hard days ahead of me. That's all.

EACH DAY YOU

STAY SOBER,

THE PAIN,

THE GUILT,

AND

THE SHAME

SLIP AWAY.

HI, MY NAME IS PARIS, AND I AM THE CHILD OF AN ADDICT.... I remember staying up all night long, laying on a tear soaked pillow, praying that my father would come home and decide what he had at home was more important than anything that he could find in the streets. It didn't happen in my time. It happened in God's time. Prayer does work; in God's perfect time. That's all.

Jesus came with forgiveness when He died for us to live. LIVE!

*

Some of us don't want our loved ones to be apart of our recovery. It feels as though, those same feelings we had when we were getting high still reside in us. We still feel the shame that kept us away from our families when we were addicts; but instead of hiding out in the crack house or on the streets, we hang out in meetings. We must let go of that shame, because if we don't invite in new feelings of hope and perseverance, we will use again. I used to tell myself that I was "doing it for myself" and that's why I was doing it by myself, however, that's the same mentality that held us captive in our selfish addicted ways and look at where that got us.

You pulled your family into your addiction, now have the courtesy to pull them into your recovery, because something we must realize is that sometimes the sinner is not the only one affected by the sin. Sometimes it is the innocent ones who are affected the most. One of my favorite parables in the Bible reflects the sentiment of shared familial sin.

There was once this great king, King David, one of the most powerful kings in all of the land. He had a trusted army of brave men and everyone knew about his exalted army; an army that walked with the favor of God, making swift defeats and grand conquests. This great king went to battle with a fierce opponent in a nearby city.

The great king was confident in his army, because although the nearby army was great, the city was much smaller. The king believed that his army was much superior. The day before he went to battle, he prayed to God and later received a vision. In the vision, God told him to kill everything and to bring nothing back. So the King went into battle against this small city, confident. However, the king and his army lost.

So the king returned and got on his knees to pray to God.

He asked, "God, why were we defeated?"

God responded saying that He told them to bring back nothing. The king proclaimed that they had done precisely as they had been instructed.

"Someone brought back something," God explained.

So the king searched out this man, and found him. The king demanded to know why he chose not to listen to the instructions. The man begged for forgiveness and gave an offering of remorse; however the king was infuriated.

The king swiftly ordered the man to bring forth his wife and child. The man did as he was instructed. Trembling, his wife and child stood there unaware of the reasons why. The king ordered for them to be killed.

God's instructions are clear. He only wants the best for our families and for our lives. In our life, when we do bad, it affects our family and they may have no idea as to why they bare the chronic weight of negative ramifications. Do your best at all times...even when you are away from your family. Let your family forever be your guiding light, when you are lost and when you are found. Continue to do God's will as often as you can.

People who are addicted to drugs have new families; the people that they do their drugs with. When the drugs run out, though, so does that new family....until next time.

FATHERHOOD FINISH LINE

MY NAME IS ROBERT BAULDWIN, AND I AM AN ADDICT... One of the things that I hate more than anything in the world is that I was not able to complete fatherhood because of my addiction. I know that God has already forgiven me for that sin, but I hope that my children can forgive me.

Fatherhood is something to be cherished. It is a gift from God and I missed out on one of His most precious gifts. I have beautiful children who had a ghost for a father, and I just pray that they forgive me. That's all.

Forgiv

eness

makes

fear

go

away

...

MY NAME IS ROBERTA, AND I AM THE CHILD OF

AN ADDICT... My heart aches often. I often find myself feeling really alone and it scares me because I have a beautiful future ahead of me and in reality I am not alone. I know God has worked some amazing miracles in my life and I believe in His promise, but sometimes I can't help but to feel the ache.

We are taught how to love by our parents. I missed that and now sometimes, trying to figure it out on my own leaves me with this ache in my heart. Maybe it's more of a pressure than an ache, but it comes often, less often these days, but it is still there. Although my father is clean and sober now, the scars still remain. I wish I had been taught how to love better, or differently rather. I wish that this ache would just go away. That's all.

*

A drunk respects no one, not even himself. In his intoxicated and impaired state, he will tear down, break up, and demolish his own domestic foundation. A drunk will influence the atmosphere with an intoxicated aroma, filling the thoughts of his loved ones with fear distress and strain causing mental suffering, which is overcome by harassment, by which he has no sympathy. The next day he may become apologetic; however, we know that a dog will always return to his vomit, plus the damage is irreparable. "Sorries" don't ease the pain of a child's aching heart, when they fear that the same will happen before supper hits the table.

A drunk wants someone to listen to him. He needs attention. He needs to be the center of everyone's attraction. "ME, ME, ME..." He is so inadequately guarded and lacks self-confidence. He lacks emotional stability, and needs someone to listen to him. He needs to be liked again, so he yells and screams and shouts at his loved ones with a frantic, familiar language. "I AM GOING TO QUIT DRINKING..."

Drunks should be diagnosed with attention deficit disorder. He's made that proclamation many times before in his life.

(Titus 2:6) Young men likewise exhort to be sober minded.

Spirit is associated with the mind, will, and feeling of the soul. If you put those fragments together with the same thought, it would equal love in the purest form; crystallizing the new world on its way in.

To have the ultimate meaning and value of existence, which is truth, is to know God.

*

MY NAME IS SUE AND I AM AN ADDICT...I am addicted to methamphetamines. Meth has destroyed my life. My children were taken away from me, because I would leave them locked in a room with no food for days. One is 11 months old and the other is four years old. They got really sick because the only thing that they would eat was their own feces and the bugs that were in the room.

They were crying one day, and someone outside called the police. When the police got there they say that they have never seen humans living like that ever; and they started looking for me. When I came around the corner, I saw the police at my house. I still had some meth left and the policeman saw me and I ran and hid so that I could hit the rest of the meth that I had. I didn't run to see if my children were okay. I didn't run to see if my children were even alive, I ran away from them...I ran away from them so I could take another hit of meth.

I lost my children over meth and my heart hurts so bad every single day knowing what kind of monster I was to my children. So I am here to try to stay sober, so that I can try and get my children back, so I can make this right. I would do anything to have my children back. I would do anything to get the moment back: the moment I first decided to get high, the moment I chose to leave them there in the closet. I will never put drugs before my children again...ever. That's all.

(Titus 2:4) That they may teach the young women to be sober, to love their husbands, and to love their children

"FOR THE WAGES OF SIN IS DEATH;

BUT THE GIFT OF GOD IS ETERNAL LIFE THROUGH

JESUS CHRIST OUR LORD." Romans 6:23

My name is Robert Bauldwin and I am an addict... I am so sorry that I started back using drugs and that I took away my children's hope. I am sorry that you were afraid of me. I am sorry for tearing things up and apart and for selling all of our stuff for dope. The more I revisit the past as I go further into my recovery, the more tears will fall. But just know...I am sorry. That's all.

THE PRICE OF PAIN

You and I have paid a lot of money to kill ourselves and hurt our families. We have paid a lot for our separation from God. In this resting place that you are in, we are going to have to deal with some things that are going to be hard to deal with, but wasn't it harder to be an addict, to sleep in unfamiliar beds and not provide for our children?

There are some things in our life that are rooted in the darkest places of our mind. We have tried to exclude painful memories of mental suffering and we retreated to drugs and alcohol. We were depressed and we didn't know it. We tried to repress memories of rape, molestation, emotional and physical abuse, or sodomy. We have to explore these memories in order to understand their implications in our addict lives, though. We have to learn to know ourselves wholeheartedly and recognize and accept any past pain, so that we can move forward and deal with the pain responsibly.

Our pasts are like shadows that stay with us, but learn to know what lurks in those shadows. It is going to be hard, but the things we want most in life are not easy to obtain; it is much harder to deal with compounding struggles while being strung out on drugs. We must have patience, and that patience has to be more than just simply staying in one place. That patience has to be defined by our mobility, even if it is gradual; we have to see the progress, while being patient for the overhaul.

The antidote for fear is **faith** in **GOD**

MY NAME IS ROBERT BAULDWIN AND I AM AN ADDICT...

When I first stopped using drugs and alcohol, it was hard. It was not because of the drugs and alcohol, but because of my thinking process. It was hard to let go of the pain of the past. So even though I was sober, I acted like I was still using. It was because my addictive life style created an obsessive-compulsive personality for me. I liked to hold onto things, especially things that were no good for me. Us addicts like the feeling of holding onto things, because in our addictive lifestyle, we tried so earnestly to hold onto our high or drunkenness. I've learned to let go. That's all I have.

Drugs make you

emotionally

and spiritually

CRIPPLED

My name is Catherine and I am an addict. I put a contract on myself because I wanted to die. I wanted to die and the dope dealer was the hit man. I paid an awful lot for the hit, and I waited a long time. Death never came; and I am so thankful that the dope dealer was not a good marks man. That's all.

*

I believe that every man or woman should have the autonomy to express a relapse back into his or her old ways. No one should have the power to take that away from them. Most people try to in attempts to make the addict feel full of shame, but by stripping the addict from confessing on their own, they are in fact taking away their salvation and making their testimony impossible to believe. Allow the addict to come clean, if a relapse occurs. Don't point the finger, because the false sense of righteousness you may feel is not only detrimental to the addict but to yourself as well.

If you relapse, don't stay out too long. Come back to recovery as soon as you can. We miss you.

THE 40 YEAR OLD SECRET

HOW COULD I TELL ANYONE?

IT WAS, AFTERALL, MY FAULT.

I LED HIM ON.

I REPEATEDLY ASKED HIM TO STOP

BUT, I LED HIM ON.

SO...YES, YES, IT WAS DEFINITLEY MY FAULT

I   SHOULD   HAVE   WORN   LESS   MAKE   UP

I DIDN'T SAY NO LOUD ENOUGH

EVERY TIME A TEAR CAME OUT,

AS I CRIED OUT,

HE HAD THE AUDACITY TO WIPE IT OFF

WHY WOULDN'T HE JUST STOP?

MY FAULT...YES MY FAULT

I SHOULD'VE SCREAMED AND KICKED HARDER

I SHOULD'VE BEEN A LITTLE SMARTER

I CAN'T LET ANYONE KNOW

BECAUSE   I   AM   NOT   A   VICTIM.   NOT ME.

I WILL BURY THIS SECRET DEEP, DEEP, DOWN IN THE ABYSS OF ME

I AM NOT A VICTIM. NO NOT ME.

MY NAME IS ROBERT BAULDWIN AND I AM AN

ADDICT... I never quite understood why I was so angry with the Omaha Public Schools (OPS). It wasn't just because they failed to educate me. There was more to my hatred. Then, during one of my therapy sessions it hit me like a lightening bolt. It began to hit me in waves and waves, which gave way to nausea, as I began to recall why I hated OPS. During that session, I began to remember accounts of being molested by Mr. Raymond Rogers, a teacher at an Omaha Public School.

I don't remember all the incidents that took place, thankfully. Your mind aids you in that fashion to help you deal with tragedy, by creating a roadblock that you have to manipulate heavily to circumnavigate. However, I do remember some of the situations in which he took advantage of me. Some of the encounters resulted in Raymond Rogers taking my feet and placing them between his legs until he ejaculated. I was 10 years old when this started, and it continued for several years.

Unfortunately, I was not the only victim; there are many of us. I am aware of at least eleven others who were molested by this teacher. Six of us have acknowledged the molestation, and in some cases the rape, and have come forward to discuss what happened in an effort to hold this man accountable for his actions.

Because of him, we have lived with these scars for more than 40 years. Some may have known him as Raymond Rogers; his victims know him as a coward who used his position as a teacher to commit crimes against boys. He lured us to his place by offering us money and to buy us clothes and shoes. Once he had our trust, he began molesting and raping us. He told us that he would give us whatever we wanted, as long as we didn't tell our friends or parents.

After 40 years, I am able to acknowledge what implications Raymond Roger's has had on my life. He only received slap on the wrist for his criminal actions, and this man preyed on innocent, poor, black boys by giving them things that he knew they wanted and could not afford. Raymond Rogers stole our innocence by raping us mentally and physically, and our lives have been drastically changed. He has yet to take responsibility for his actions. I will be sure every day to take responsibility for mine. That's all.

*

Some of us have experienced pain so deep and wide that it is hard to imagine how we survived, but we did. God brought us through, so that we could share our testimony. I will never know or understand why evil exists, why children get sick, why predators chose to destroy lives; but I will always understand God's unyielding LOVE and FAVOR. If we chose to live by HIS WILL, we will have access to a light so bright that it covers even the darkest areas of our heart and the most malice sin and injustice.

There are some people who really want to speak out against the ills of the world and do not because they are afraid of altering their position in life. There are many victims that suffer in silence, because it is far better to wear a mask, than it is to wear the title of victim, as though it is a scarlet letter, by which they will be judged. Being a victim does not make you weak; it makes you strong, because you have survived. No one tells the office worker who made it out of the Twin Tower that he is weak, because he was a victim that tragic day. No one looks down at the soldier who has had both of his legs amputated in the war, with any less pride. It is a shame what happens to the strength of a person, more concerned with their position, than with justice; the justice that comes from speaking out against your accuser.

Well, I have a position in heaven waiting for me and I am willing to bet it is a lot better than any position held here on earth. I choose to speak up against transgression, and I choose to soberly speak against addiction.

We all will revisit our pasts. Just don't let it take control of you. We have to revisit our pasts so that we can have some sort of ammunition for what is to come in front of us. Stay sober. Don't let the shadow become what defines your identity. Let the shadow be what follows behind as you march into your destiny, always remembering, but never wavering.

(Colossians 3:8-10) But now ye also put off all these; anger, wrath, malice, blasphemy, filthy communication out of your mouth. 9Lie not one to another, seeing that ye have put off the old man with his deeds; 10And have put on the new man, which is renewed in knowledge after the image of him that created him:

COMPROMISE AND COMMUNICATION

In recovery compromises are necessary, if not, then our recovery life will be just like our addictive life. We will have joy after attending a meeting because we will feel better that we were able to talk about being sober. We will, also, have joy stepping into the crack house. We will have sorrow when we miss a meeting because we were passed out on the floor of the crack house. We will have sorrow the moment we are unable to go to the crack house. There will not be a middle ground. No gray area to ponder in. It's either black or white: joy or sorrow. Compromise is where healing comes from. Compromises are necessary in recovery. Understanding that compromise is necessary is necessary.

If your wife wants to spend time together tonight...do it. It's simple. If your children want to spend time with you today.... do it. It's simple. A.A meetings have been around since 1935 and will continue to exist. Compromise for your family, it is good for your recovery.

Your   family   comes   first   in   recovery.

MY NAME IS ROBERT BAULDWIN AND I AM AN ADDICT...I went to a meeting the other day, and I heard this guy say that his family and church didn't understand him the way that the people in the meeting did. I didn't really agree with that. Church and AA are the same. The church is one big rehab center. People go to church to find out why they keep doing wrong and how to fix it.

People go to alcoholics anonymous for the same reason. Drunks go to church. Crack heads go to church. Prostitutes go to church. They all go to church, just like they all go to meetings. We go to AA meetings and tell people that we do not know all about our problems, just like confessions in church. We go to both places and tell strangers how we stole food from our family. Our family knows. They went days without food. We tell them how we used to beat our wife. She knows. She still has the bruises and a broken arm. The point is, our families know us better than any of these strangers. They know us better than the stranger that resides inside of us, that we ourselves don't even know.

We cannot seek sympathy in the AA room, but betray our family and continuously throw them under speeding buses. That's not recovery.

God

Is

Love...

Love yourself.

My name is Paris Bauldwin and I am the child of an addict. I was so upset at God for a long, long time. I didn't understand how he could put such a good heart in such a bad man. I knew my dad was doing the best that he could, because he had a good heart, but he continued to make the worst decisions for himself and his family. He was a good man; I knew deep down he was. The days when he would tutor kids in the neighborhood, or come out and play kickball with us in the yard... My favorite memories from my childhood are of him, front row at our Christmas plays, with his disposable camera, standing, snapping away. He was a good man...he was a good man with a great heart. He instilled that goodness inside of me. I got my dad's tough hair and resilient heart.

So silly to think, that I could have ever been mad at God for teaching me the single most important lesson of my life. I see people for the character of their heart, not the result of their actions, because benevolence resides in us all. How could I ever be mad at God for teaching me the single best lesson of my life, every day of my life? That's all.

An addict's favorite words are ' I love' and ' I am sorry'. You can't love anyone, without first loving yourself.

My name is Robert Bauldwin and I am an addict....There is a book that I read everyday. My wife gave it to me as a gift a long time ago and I pick it up every single day. It is called, "My Utmost For His Highest". I was reading the book the other day, and it said that child of God is not conscious of the will of God because he or she is the will of God. So to the newcomer, this should help you out with the *will* of God. His *will* is you. Stay sober. That's all.

ADMISSION FOR TWO

In recovery, we admit, we believe, we make a decision. However, we must also listen to others' confessions. It is difficult for an addict to listen. We are inherently selfish and not listening is a trait that we found comfort in; not listening to our mother's pleas for us to come home, not listening to our fathers or brothers or sisters...not listening to our children as they cried and begged us to not go out and use. We didn't even listen to that silent voice in our head that told us about the regret we would feel after we used.

In recovery we must listen. Judge Judy said that God gave us two ears and one mouth, to listen twice and speak once. As much as I don't like judges, she is so very right.

*

HELLO, MY NAME IS ROBERT BAULDWIN AND I AM AN ADDICT...I used to think that my life was bad, until I was listening to this woman tell her story. She said when she was eight years old she had to go and live with her grandparents. Her grandparents were hooked on drugs. At night, her grandparents would come and sneak into her room. Her grandmother would hold her down, while her grandfather raped her. They did this to this woman every night, and she explained with tears in her eyes, how one night while her grandfather was on top of her, her grandmother put a pillow over her face. She eventually passed out and her grandparents figured she was dead, so they took her out into the backyard, dug a hole, and put her in it. They covered her with dirt and left her for dead.

Staring at her hands, she explained how when she woke up she began digging her way out of the grave. She told everyone how she didn't know if God was with her or not; all she knew was that He did not help her when she was screaming out for Him to come. She began crying as she said how every since that day she had been digging herself out of a hole. That's all I have.

(Genesis 3:11) The just shall live by faith.

When you get a thought that you want to use drugs, all you have to do is turn to the Bible. In the book of James, it reminds us to submit ourselves to God. Resist the devil and he will flee from you. **(James 4:10)** Humble yourselves in the sight of the Lord and He shall lift you up.

All things are possible with God.

GET A PLANT...AND A CLUE

In recovery, we are told not to get into relationships, that we should get to know ourselves. We are instructed to get a plant, or a dog, but steer clear of relationships. Well, I didn't have that luxury. I was in and out of what seemed to be shot gun relationships; you know the kind you have with bill and debt collectors. Sometimes its really rocky, sometimes it is extremely hostile and downright nasty. Like with bill collectors, though, the reflection of the relationship's existence manifested itself as a present tangible object, the distance and hostility from never really "paying" for what I had caused all the problems.

The times when I just wanted to reach out and touch someone or wave the white flag and surrender where negated by the reality that I never paid my bills. There were nights when I would just sit in the middle of a dark room and cry. There was no empathy or sympathy for me, because I was the broken element that caused for the relationship to remain stuck in the mud. I had to divorce myself from these sort of emotionally distressed relationships. I got to "pay my bills" in recovery. It'll break me, but I know the reformed new me can afford it.

People in recovery are recovering from something, which denotes that we are sick. Two sick thinking people cannot get into a relationship. The stealthy disease will eventually find cracks to sneak through, so get a plant, water it daily, love it, and begin to pay your dues.

Beware of the dangers of relaxation in your spiritual walk with recovery. Weariness is a tool that the devil uses repeatedly and stealthily without our knowledge of its presence.

For this is the will of God, even your sanctification, that ye should abstain from fornication.   (1 Thessalonians 4:3)

So to the newcomer, this means don't get into that new relationship, because you crave feeling. Don't use A.A as a dating game, especially those of you that have spouses at home. While you are here, take the first step, which is controlling your vessel: your temple, your body.

MY NAME IS PARIS BAULDWIN AND I AM THE DAUGHTER OF AN ADDICT. I used to think my life was bad, until I awakened on a sunny day

in Atlanta in August of 2005 and watched as people sat on their rooftops, uncertain if they'd be rescued from the flooding and devastation left after Hurricane Katrina hit New Orleans. I sat in tears, watching as families were ripped apart and homes and hopes were destroyed. Sure, in my life, I have seen some pretty tough times, but this was horrific and heart wrenching.

My parents separated when I was young, and the only images I have of them together are ones filled with blood and fighting...not a single one of them smiling together. Sure I lived in and out of homeless shelters due to my father's addiction. Sure I've struggled with loving myself at times, because at times it felt that the two people who are supposed to love me the most (my parents) didn't, but God gave me resilience, serenity, and an inherent ability to persevere.

The person I am today would not exist had I never slept on the chilling wooden floor of a house with no electricity, or cried myself to sleep listening to my father's screams as he withdrew from cocaine, in the single bedroom we shared at a small family shelter in Peoria.

On that sunny day in August, I saw the true faces of real victims. I realized I was never a victim at all. I realized then and now that I am simply a bi product of situations that tested my faith and built my character. That's all I have.

In recovery alcoholics tend

to make their problems

BIGGER than what they really

are. In recovery, be true to yourself.

<u>LOVE, HONOR AND OBEY</u>

This preacher said that his wife would always pester him to tell her how much she loved him. One day, he got extremely exhausted by his wife's tenacious requests. She pestered him the same as she did day after day, and he told her to come to him. He pointed at the TV and said, "I got that for you". He pointed towards the kitchen, " He said, I provide for you." He pointed out the window to their brand new car in the driveway. "You see that car, I paid that off for you. Now," he exclaimed, "I can take it all back, I can stop providing for you in the way that I do, and tell you that I love you."

In recovery,

love must be

deeds and actions

†

Spoken words of affection are constantly negated by actions that speak louder and to the contrary. You do not have to tell someone you love them...just love them.

If there is no vision in recovery, you will walk through your recovery, and never stay there.

*My name is Robert Bauldwin and I am an addict...*The reason that I say I am an addict is because it connects me with my addictive life. This way it doesn't control me, I control it. I choose not to believe in the disease philosophy. It makes me feel like I am completely deteriorating away. Recovery means to recover. There are some people who come to A.A meetings who are afraid to say that they believe another way, some believe that it is not a sickness, that you will never be healed, because after all, recovery means to be made whole again. So how can you be in recovery forever? Not to get into all that. I believe in the power of choice that God gave me to know right from wrong. No matter what you believe, it is the fellowship that means something. So keep coming back. I will be here. That's all.

We must be inspired and persistent in our recovery.

PRICELESS PERSISTENCE

We must be inspired and persistent in our recovery, in the same fashion we were in our addictive life. We worked so hard in that life, with one goal in mind. We were so determined, so focused on getting high. We thought about it every minute of every day. We would lie, steal and cheat for drugs. We would even steal from our own children, cheat our parents, and lie to the ones we loved. It was a hard job; a very taxing one and it had no benefits. We should use that same physical and emotional fortitude in our recovery. Be persistent.

To the newcomer, I want you to take this to heart and hold onto it. Never allow yourself to mimic or feign your commitment just to feel acceptance. It's not enough to simply wait on the Lord's will. You may attempt to convince yourself that is what rehab is about so that you can feel included...accepted, but it is going to take a lot of hard work and persistence. Most of our lives, we have been told that we were going to be nothing, no one was ever going to want us...love us. We have been raped, molested, humiliated, degraded. It's time to reclaim our lives. Greater is HE that is in us, than he that is in all of the world.

Tell yourself that you have made a good and upstanding decision not to use. Remind yourself to think positively about yourself. Allow the acceptance you seek to begin with you, because it is a guarantee that in our new recovery we will feel acceptance. It's been a long time since someone wanted to be around us, so we will want to tell him or her all about ourselves. Stop, that's not necessarily the wisest thing to do. Remember, the people confined in those four walls of those meetings are sick thinking people. Some things are best kept between you and God. Seek persistently within yourself, the acceptance you desire from others. God heals all, anyway, in the presence or absence of men. Remember that in recovery.

*

This man, new in his recovery, wanted to make amends with his wife. He said he had a spiritual awakening. It's funny, that's what all newcomers think; however, they should just become spiritually aware of the knowledge of what true indemnity means. He wanted to tell her that he slept with her sister. He was warned against it because it would really hurt her. He told her anyway. She left him. He is off somewhere getting drunk. Good for him, right?

Sometimes the best words are the ones that don't get spoken. Sometimes silence is the best answer.

MY NAME IS ROBERT BAULDWIN AND I AM AN ADDICT... I never had many possessions or many people to make amends to; all I had was my family, my children who loved me, and my first book, "Letters From an Addictive Child". I lost it all the drugs and alcohol. That's all I have.

If you tell yourself

you will go one mile

in recovery,

tell yourself to go **TWO**.

Take the extra mile in recovery.

My name is Paris Bauldwin and I am the child of a recovering addict... In April of 2007, my home burned to the ground. I lost everything, including the money from my student loan check that I had just cashed and stashed in a jewelry box in my bedroom. My sister and I were living in a three-bedroom condo in Atlanta. We were so excited when we found this incredible place, because it was a rarity and had three bathrooms, as well, so we wouldn't have to share. Trust me, to us girls, it meant the world.

The rent was incredible, especially compared to what I am paying now living in Los Angeles. I am actually paying the same amount for a one bedroom currently that we were paying for a three-bedroom, three bathroom, two story, updated condo, but I digress.

We were renters and did not think that it was necessary to have renter's insurance, at the time. My older brother and sister lived with us, and my younger brother and his best friend, and his best friend's girlfriend also inhabited the location. My sister and I worked long hours, night and day to maintain the place, not only our sake, but also that of our family that perpetually depended on us, so at the bare minimum, the stress of not having to share a bathroom...that often, took a bit of the edge off.

I was at work when I received the call that I needed to come home, because our home was on fire. I rushed home to find, not only was our home on fire, but it was engulfed in flames and nearly burned entirely to the ground. I cried, not because of the things that I lost, but because of the fear in starting completely over from scratch. My sister was 8 months pregnant, and my brothers and sisters, as well as myself, were now homeless. Nothing we haven't faced before, but it hurt.... again...it hurt. My mother came along after the ashes had settled. I felt helpless. I realized the worthlessness of material things and appreciated the value in people so much more. We were able to rebound, but there is still some scar tissue. That's all I have.

(1 Corinthians 2:5)

That your faith

should not stand in

the wisdom of men,

but in the power of

GOD

Get better, please, we need you.

THE SOBER SHUFFLE

Struggling in sobriety is a good thing. It means that you will arduously engage in trying to find a solution to the problem, enabling sobriety in your life. If there is no struggle there is no progress. It's like a woman giving birth. There is a progression she has to go through. She has to push through struggles and pain.

Push. Struggle. Progress. Push. Pain. Struggle. Progress... then the baby is born. The pain goes away and becomes the joy of new life. In our recovery, our pain will go away because of the joy in our new recovery life.

In recovery, if we understand the pain, this will enable us to grow out of pain. It's called growing pains. Remember the pain in the addictive life. You never have to use drugs again. I have proof. I was at a meeting and there was over 150 years of sobriety. Understand and remember the pains, and push through to your new life. Jesus made it plain and simple for us to understand.

Persistence is being truthful, faithful and upright with our morality.

MY NAME IS ROBERT BAULDWIN AND I AM AN ADDICT. You know I want to stop using, but the only time I want to stop is when I have no money. I want to learn how to stop when I have money. I want to be able to have a wallet full of money and not be urged to spend it on drugs or alcohol. It is hard. That's all.

In recovery seek ye the kingdom of God. Just ask and it shall be given to you. Seek and you shall find. Knock and the beautiful doors of your brilliant future will open like floodgates, ushering you into your best and brightest days.

I think in my addiction I kept asking myself, would Jesus do this?

DIRTY DRIVING

Drinking alcohol and getting drunk does not defile a man. He just looks silly and acts very stupidly, but when a man begins to violently beat and/or threaten his wife with physical and mental harm; that defiles a man, those are things that come from his heart. It didn't just arrive when he was drunk; it was always present.

Defile means to dirty or pollute. This is what that man that beats you looks like on the inside, dirty, polluted, and filthy. However, most women only see the smile and facade that encases the filth. If a man hits you once, he will hit you again. He will make up an excuse why he hit you and apologize. He will tell you he was under the influence of alcohol. That's a lie. He hit you because he never loved you; matter of a fact, he hates you. How could he love you? He doesn't even love himself.

Matthew 15:18

> **But those things which**
>> **proceed out of the mouth**
>>> **come from the heart and defile a man.**

My name is Robert Bauldwin and I am an addict... Sometime ago, I became a hard-core junkie. There was a time right after I had gotten paid, I gave my daughter some money, and then I went and purchased some dope with the remaining money. I checked into a motel around one or two in the morning, and I called my daughter, because I really wanted the money back because all my dope was gone.

She was just 13 years old. I was in a very bad part of town, paranoid and afraid to leave the room. She got out of bed and caught a cab to come to where I was. I watched her walk up the stairs. I could feel all her insecurities, all of her fear, all of the hurt in her heart. I knew it was painful for her to have to watch her father deteriorate to nothing. She handed me the money and told me that she would do anything for me to get better. She told me with tears swelling in her eyes that she loved me. That kind of unconditional love that comes from a child that loves their parent is God like love. I walked away from it.

She told me that she had spoken to her mother and that she was going to take her younger brother and leave to go and stay with her for a while. She paused waiting for me to respond and tell her that I loved her and that I didn't want her to leave, that I would get better. She paused there on the stairs of this dirty motel at 3 am and waited for me to reach out and hug her and be a father, and reassure that our lives would be better; but I said nothing.

As the tears that were mounting in her eyes began to fall, she told me how she had arranged a ride to Georgia from Illinois and that they were leaving the next day. I just stood there and watched as my precious little girl's heart was torn to pieces. I did nothing to comfort her. She hugged me, told me that she loved me and left.

After she left, I went and bought some crack. When it was all gone and the reality set in, I called for them and realized they were really gone. My heart stopped beating and I died...I died in that very moment on the inside. There was no good inside of me, and I wanted God to just kill me right where I stood.

In my heart, I so badly wanted my children back, but in my soul I didn't want them to see me killing myself. That turmoil stirred in me like a category five hurricane, so I walked into a building, went to the top floor, climbed out the window, and stood on the edge. I stared down five stories to what would most certainly be my death, and thought about my children; how they smiled, how happy they were when they played. I thought about how I was supposed to be their protector, the one they felt safe with, and since I failed them, I felt that I should just die.

I looked up to God and asked Him to forgive me; someone pulled me back into the window. I do not know who it was. All I know is that God gave me another chance to be a father...to be a better man. That's all I have

Love for your children=love for yourself.

In recovery we must

turn every negative

into a positive. Love will

always do that.

My name is Paris Bauldwin and I am the child of an addict... One day, when I was 13 years old, I felt what it was like to feel complete and tangible, unbearable pain. My father, the man who was supposed to love me the most in this world, said without saying that he loved dope more than he loved me.

We were homeless, again, and living with my father's estranged father, who detested us. Frank, my father's father, had walked out on my nana when my father and his six brothers and sister were still small. However, on one cold night, my father decided that he was going to drive from Nebraska to Illinois in the dead of winter so that he, my younger brother Chris and I, could start a new life with the help of his father.

I remember being frightened out of my mind as we drove in this beat up blue station wagon, with no heat, on icy roads. My father was drinking, and I thought, for sure, we would end up in a ditch somewhere and that the snow would cover us, and no one would ever find out bodies until the snow thawed in the Spring. But somehow, with God's grace, we made it. But the nightmare of the car ride to Peoria didn't end with our arrival.

My "grandfather" seemed happy enough to see us, but he would soon show us otherwise, by making snide comments about our father's drug addiction and overall making us feel unwanted. I remember one day after school, coming to his house and him yelling from the top of the stairs about us needing to find our father who had been missing, cause we needed to leave.

I ran out of the front door and looked for my dad. I went to these projects that were near by and cried as I wondered aimlessly. I remember not wanting to step foot back in that man's house. I thought that if I could find my daddy and tell him, he would surely take us back to Nebraska and realize that he *HAD* to get right.

I saw a man that claimed to know my father, and he told me about this house he had seen him in. He gave me directions, and as I walked, I prepared this speech in my head that would touch my father's soul and make him want to stop using, for our sake. When I got to the house this woman, high out of her mind, answered the door and told me my father was dead and started laughing. I began crying and she told me she was only joking and that she hadn't seen him.

I went back to my "grandfather's" house and sat in the computer room closest to the door, so as not to be detected. I stayed there all day, and I cried as I heard my "grandfather" talk terribly about our presence and about our no good dad. My father showed up some time later. He snuck in and saw me sitting there. He wanted to go unnoticed so he quickly came in, paranoid and constantly looking out the windows; he didn't even notice I was crying. He gave me some money and left, no hello, no goodbye, just some jumbled "you guys okay?" with no sincerity behind it.

My grandfather came in the room shortly after, because he heard me crying. He just stared at me and told me that I needed to call my mother, because we couldn't stay there any longer. I called my mother. I told her that we didn't have any place to go, and she said she would try and figure out a way to get us from Peoria to Atlanta.

Later that night, I met my father at a dirty motel and that is when he said without saying, that he loved dope more than my siblings and me. I left completely broken that night and rode down to Georgia with a complete stranger, to see another complete stranger, my mother. That's all I have.

FREE FALL

Some of us don't want our love ones to be apart of our recovery; we say "I have to do it for myself, by myself." But, isn't that the same type of thinking we had in our addictive life? We were self-seekers and self-doers, but our addiction was not our own. We dragged them into our addiction, leaving them with no option. Now it is only courteous to pull them into our recovery. We don't really have the option to deny them this victory.

In our addictive life we fed on hatred and destruction. We devastated and plundered anything from our family and left our loved ones destitute, but we have the audacity to go to rehab claiming that we ourselves have hit rock bottom .We have left our families falling in free fall from our habitual, inept behavior. In our recovery we must get rid of the "I's" and embrace the "We's", because we addicts didn't go through our addictive life without spreading our destruction. We have to embrace the "we" and get our families out of the free fall and back on solid ground.

Every time I think about the tears in my children's eyes because of my addiction, my heart cries out for forgiveness.

MY NAME IS ROBERT BAULDWIN AND I AM AN

ADDICT... I remember the week before I would get paid, I would tell myself, "I am going to go home and do the right thing: pay my bills, buy my children groceries, the things a parent is supposed to do when caring for his children".

I would go and get all cleaned up on pay day, and I would tell myself that I just needed one hit, and then I would head home to do the right thing. It never worked out that way.

I would go into the crack house looking like prince charming and leave looking like the ugly duckling. It would seem like I was there for at least a day, but in reality it was only five hours, and all the money I had was gone. I had paid no bills nor bought any groceries and I was afraid to go home; a grown man afraid to go home. That is what drugs do to us, they steal our backbone; and when I would walk through the doors of my house, I would abuse those favored words "love" and "sorry".

With tears in their eyes, my children would retreat back into the darkness of the cold house. They would eat rice, because Daddy didn't buy any food because he stopped at the dope house first. They would spend yet another night going to bed hungry and cold because I didn't do the right thing. That's all.

SECRET'S SOCIETY

Society would like you to think that the dope dealer makes all of the money. Well, he makes some of the money, and it isn't as glorious as it is on television. Yes, the dope dealer's children have brand new clothes; while mine have hand me downs and their shoes have holes in them. Yes the dope dealer drives a new fancy car, while I have no car and my children take the bus to school, but he doesn't make all of the money.

I went into a store, and as soon as I walked in, I saw a crack kit on the counter. There was a lighter, a pipe, fancifully decorated with a rose inside of it, and a box full of griddles. I thought to myself, this is more than enough paraphernalia to get someone some "more than a enough" time behind bars; but, then I also thought about how the company that makes the lighter makes money off of the crack head. The company that makes the nice pipes, with the enticing roses, makes money off of the crack head, and the company that makes the griddle makes money off of the crack head. Everybody makes money off of the addict, everyone except the addict.

Mahatma Gandhi said, "Almost everything you do will seem insignificant, but it is important that you do it". Look at how putting together the individual fragments will affect piecing this thing called life together. Stay sober. Love your family. Love your life.

FEAR IS CREATED WHEN WE DO BAD

THINGS TO OUR LOVED ONES.

IT IS HARD TO FACE THEM

WHEN THERE IS NO FOOD IN THE HOUSE.

IT IS HARD TO

FACE THEM WHEN THE LIGHTS ARE OFF.

IT IS HARD TO FACE THEM

WHEN THE RENT ISN'T PAID.

My name is Stephen and I am an addict...I want to thank God for loving me, until I was able to love myself. My drug addicted self, didn't want to love me, and if I couldn't love myself, it was impossible to think that anyone else could love me...but God never stopped. Thank YOU!

† *Faith comes by hearing the word of God.*

SILLY, SILLY RABBIT

Why have hell on earth, when you can have a little bit of heaven right here on earth? On the doors of every rehab center here in America, there should be a sign that all addicts must read that says, " I am 'so and so', I can not say the words 'I love you' nor 'I am sorry' as long as I am in this rehab, because love plus sorry equals an emotion".

Addicts favor emotions. This is how we get back into the house, back into the grace of our families, back into the hearts of the ones we have hurt, with an emotion. At the rehab center, we are taught to show our love with deeds and actions. We are enabled to show our love without saying those simple three words.

*

The wage of sin is death, and we pay a great deal to kill ourselves, with drugs and alcohols and various avenues that lead us into sin. The Lord told Jonah to go and preach to Nineveh. Jonah did not like them, so Jonah paid the fare to flee to a place called Tarshish, so that he could depart from the presence of the Lord. How silly was Jonah? The Lord prepared a great fish to swallow Jonah, something Jonah could have never foreseen nor predicted.

Now when Jonah was in the belly of the fish, he did the same thing us addicts do when all of the money is gone. The lights are turned off, and our children sit famished in our faces; he cried out to the Lord. How often do we try to flee the presence of the Lord, only to find ourselves crying out for him in once we are in the belly of the beast?

My name is Robert Bauldwin and I am an alcoholic.... I want you to know that I have been to a lot of rehabs. I have been to a ten-month rehab, a six-month rehab, a 33-day rehab and a one-day rehab. Upon my arrival from these rehabs, hoping to be greeted with open arms, I'd enter into my home and say "Honey, I'm home," and she'd reply, "Honey, I'm gone."

You see, our family wants for us to do well. I mean, some of them do, and some of them don't give a damn, but those that do, want us to go to rehab and stay for a while, so that they can experience tranquility in the hours, or days we are gone. Similarly, if we go to jail, they experience that same sense of relief.

They want you to be locked up, in rehab or jail, so that you cannot get out and sneak into the house when they are asleep and steal from them, or scare them when you don't come home at night. There is a stillness in their hearts, in knowing that you are safe from harm and they are safe from hurt, even if it is only for a day or a month. So, as tough as it may be for you, stay a while in rehab, not only for you, but for your family to relish in stolen tranquility.

In recovery you need to stop reminiscing with the past. The only reason we have to look back is so that we can aid something foreseen in front of us. ***That is recovery.***

HI, MY NAME IS BETTY AND I AM NOT AN

ALCOHOLIC... I am 90 years old. I walked into my house, and my 48 year old son was on the floor picking up little pieces of God knows what. He would put the debris into his pipe and attempt to smoke it. When that didn't work, I am ashamed to say, but he went to the kitty litter and began putting that into his pipe. I knew then he had departed from the reality that he once knew, and I knew then, that the only way I could provide any assistance to him would be from a distance. I never thought that any drugs could make a man act like that. I asked him to leave the next day. That's all I have.

(1 Thessalonians 5:6-8) Therefore, let us not sleep as do others, but let us watch and be sober.

For they that sleep in the night and they that be drunken are drunken in the night.

But let us, who are of the day, be sober, putting on the breastplate of faith and love and a helmet, the hope of salvation.

CHRISTMAS CRAFTS

A child's mind is carefully crafted. It is programmed to love in the same perfect way that God loves. However, as parents, we are in control of how we develop that love. So it is confusing to a child who loves his parent unconditionally, to have to question why that love is not reciprocated in that same unconditional manner. Is this love, mom, when you beat me down and the next ay you say you say you love me? Is this love, dad, when you say you love me and don't come home at night? Is this love, mom, when you are too high to come and pick me up from school, so I sit there as the sun sets with tears in my eyes? Is this love, dad, when you sell our Christmas gifts on Christmas Eve, so we waken to pine needles and an empty floor where gifts used to reside?

*

My name is Paris, and I am the child of an addict... I remember growing up, how special Christmases were to me. They were very special, because every year we would participate in the Christmas programs at our schools. My father would attend. I remember one Christmas program playing "Ode to Joy" as the opening of the program. My father was in the front row cheering me on, and taking pictures.

There is something truly invaluable in a parent's pride in their children. It makes a child desire to succeed. My father used to attend all of our programs and take pictures, and before the programs he would take us shopping for dresses and suits to wear so that we would sparkle onstage. Somewhere we lost our sparkle, though.

It was so hard deciphering which father to love. I know he was one man, but the man that attended our Christmas programs and the man at home were two different people. The belligerent drunk who would get into fights with my older brother and the man behind the camera at the Christmas programs were two very different people.

I loved both with the perfect love of God, but it was so hard deciphering between the two. Especially, when the programs were over and Christmas break begun, and we were at home all day for those vacation weeks, most of it was spent in nervous anxiety about where food was going to come from and if our Christmas gifts would remain underneath the tree before Christmas came.

Christmas is still a very special time for me. It is a time to create new memories and a reminder of the beauty of second chances. We are given a new time every year to create new and special memories. The good Christmas memories are more prevalent than the bad ones, and I don't know if that is because as we get older our memories flee us or because it is God's plan for me to live life abundantly. Either way, I am thankful that on Christmas now, I don't have to decipher between which man to love. I know who is coming to dinner at Christmas, my wonderfully, sober father, with his camera, ready to take a few pictures. That's all

We were

taught

as children to

keep secrets.

We are told

"what

happens in

this

house

stays in this

house".

My name is

Robert Bauldwin

and I am an addict...

Dear my beautiful children,

Thank you for never

giving up on me...

That's All

Another day and another season.

Today I defeat, completely and decisively. I won the battle. I didn't use.

PAPER, PLASTIC, OR SOBRIETY?

There are three pertinent ideas in the AA book. Number three says that God could and would, if He was sought. Sought means to go out and find. It is an action word, which means you have to do something. YOU have to do something. Sobriety does not just walk up to you in the grocery store. Sobriety doesn't come with the morning milk. You have to decide to go out and seek sobriety. You have to go out and seek the happiness that your family deserves. **YOU** have to, so **GOD** can. The kingdom of God is within you. Start SEEKING inside yourself. That's where you will find HIM.

Be *good* to yourself

in recovery.

Be *good* to GOD.

My name is Paris Bauldwin and I am the child of an addict...I recently had a talk with someone who said they didn't believe in God. They told me that the Bible was full of stories and fiction. I looked at them in their eyes and told them my testimony. You see, you can debate religion all day, but testimony is a proven FACT. God saved me. God gave me my father back. God continues to purpose my steps and that's REALITY, not fiction or farce. That's all.

This is the will of God,
that we faithfully love
God with all of our heart, mind,
body and soul, and that we

do the righteous,

justifiable, praiseworthy deed.

We cannot put our recovery on lay away until it is convenient for us.

My name is Robert Bauldwin and I am an addict... The best part of writing this book is that I get to walk with God every day. So if you want to walk with God, just tell your story.

> 13And it shall turn to you for a testimony. 14Settle it therefore in your hearts, not to meditate before what ye shall answer: 15For I will give you a mouth and wisdom, which all your adversaries shall not be able to gainsay nor resist. **(Luke 21:13-15)**

The truth of your testimony will set you free, and the flesh is aware of this and that is way the flesh has waged a war against your spirit. I remember as a little boy, I would go to church, and rarely did I pay attention. Much of my attention was centered on the pretty little girls there and not much on what was being said, but I do remember the preacher constantly saying, "tell the truth and shame the devil."

God put it in your heart to come forth and give a testimony; don't doubt it, because a doubtful minded person is unstable in all of their ways. Embrace sharing your testimony. The heavens will send out aid to someone who hears it and is made whole again. You are not alone in your journey to sobriety, so reach out and share your testimony. It will bring you closer to God. You won't be able to escape the healing power of sharing. You will be healed, and you may just help someone else heal, as well. So stand up and give your testimony. Tell the truth and shame the devil. That is all.

Be not drunk with wine wherein excess, but be filled with the spirit.

(EPHESIANS 5:18)

MR. A.A

My name is Jim and I am an addict... When I was in rehab, I met this guy. You know how easy it is to meet people in rehab and some people just stay with you, you know. This guy really just stuck out. He was in rehab for about two weeks.

Inside of the walls of rehab, it is usually pretty simple to spot the counterfeits from those genuinely seeking help, because at some point or another, we addicts have played the role of both. Anyway, this guy was always in his A.A book and his 12 Step book, and I mean all of the time. He even got a sponsor. Other people in rehab would go to him for advice, because he really seemed to jump into his recovery headfirst.

I knew something was up with, Minister A.A, though. Most men, after one day, call home begging and crying to their wives or girlfriends. He went two weeks. I was guessing that he had to get his courage up or something.

Well one day, I see him walking towards the phone. He was walking really slowly too, like he was walking to his execution or something. Perhaps in his mind he was walking to the execution of his relationship. So anyway, he picks up the phone and called someone.

His expression began to change. He was started looking kind of crazy. Whoever was on the other line was not saying what he wanted to hear. So this is where it gets good; he was calling home for the first time in two weeks. From what I could gather, his wife had been worried sick about him for the past two weeks. Her and the kids thought he was dead. They couldn't find him or their car and hadn't heard from him.

She explained to him how her and their kids had spent the last two weeks in tears, thinking the worst. He told her he had been in rehab. There was a pause in their conversation and she replied with "You've been where?"

"Rehab," he repeated.

"Why are you there?" she asked.

"Well, baby I felt so bad that I couldn't stop using," he lowered his tone a little.

"Using what?" she inquired.

His voice softened to a child's whisper. "I've been using crack for about six years. I wanted to get help."

"So you've been an undercover crack head," she responded, patience worn thin.

"No, I am not a crack head," he replied. "I just needed help to stop that's all. I love you and I am sorry you had to find out like this. But I found out why I am here. I have a disease."

Angry now his wife responded, "DISEASE! I slept with you very recently and I am fine. The kids are fine...what kind of disease are you talking about?" She paused in her speech. "Oh, you mean you have a crack disease. Is that supposed to make everything better."

Now he was getting really uncomfortable, people were looking at him and she was yelling really loud on the other line, so everybody could hear.

"Baby, I didn't call you to make you upset. I just wanted to let you know that I am okay. I just wanted to let you know where I am. I wish I would have been hurt. It would have been easier to tell the children that, then to tell them that their dad is a crack head."

He paused, at a lost for words and leaned against the wall.

"I have to ask you something," anger fleeting from her voice.

It sounded like she was softening up a little, like she was becoming more understanding; so we all thought that our free entertainment for the afternoon was over.

Trembling he responded to her request, "Yes baby, ask whatever. Please...anything."

"What did you do with our car...our 50,000 dollar car, that the police can't find."

Interrupting, "I will get that back. I promise. I will get that back."

"And your job? How do you plan on getting that back?

"Baby, please..."

"No. You don't call here, or send any mail or anything, until you tell me how much crack you got for that car."

She slammed the phone down, and as much as I wanted to walk away and pretend that I wasn't listening to their conversation, I stood there and watched as Mr. AA stood listening to the dial tone.

He started pacing back and forth and back and forth, and then he began talking to himself, because insecurity started settling in and it was uncomfortable to him. He started telling himself that his wife was wrong to not be so unforgiving, for not understanding, and that he was right.

He started assassinating the character of his wife, trying to convince himself that she was ungodly. One of the nearby spectators told him that he needed to call his sponsor, but he just kept going on and on until finally he realized he needed to call his sponsor. So he picked up the phone, and I wanted to grab some popcorn because I knew that this was going to be good.

Once his sponsor picked up the phone, he went on and on about how his wife was getting on his nerves, saying all she ever thinks about is money. His sponsor then tells him that it would be a great idea if he didn't call his wife for 30 days. He didn't like that. He inquired about wanting to talk to his children, and his sponsor told him that he didn't think about his children when he was looking for crack, so give it 30 days.

Mr. AA didn't like being told what to do, so he stormed out and made his way out of rehab, deciding that he would just go home and face the music. However, first he stopped at the crack house, got high. When he got home, his wife wasn't having that foolishness around her children and called the police. He got arrested and that marriage got sent to funeral home to be put to rest. That's all I have.

Alcohol and drugs are a very small part of **addiction.**

The smallest decision in life often holds significance & weighted consequence; and the decision to stop using drugs and drinking alcohol is one of those decisions; small but torrential.

MY NAME IS ROBERT BAULDWIN AND I AM AN ADDICT... Today at the meeting, they talked about acceptance. Most people in AA think all they have to do is have acceptance without using or drinking, and if they do that, they will find the gold in the pot at the end of the rainbow. There is more to staying sober than simply gaining acceptance and abstaining from drug use.

To accept, you cannot misuse your wife anymore. You have to accept that God is a living God and you have to accept that you cannot use bad language. In Romans 12:2-3, it tells us,

> 2 Be not conformed to this world but be ye transformed by the renewing of your mind. 3 That ye may prove what is that good and acceptable and perfect will of God.

So there are a lot of things in our addictive life that we will have to accept, but in order to stay sober we must accept God. Simply acknowledging that He exists is not enough. We must accept Him, wholly as He has accepted us wholly, flaws and all. That's all.

But unto every one of us is given grace according to the measure of the gift of Christ. So, you have grace from God. What is it that you fear? With God's grace you can go anywhere and do anything. Believe in yourself and take flight.

Now that I am sober, I am still poor, but not drunk.

ADAM AND EVENTUALLY

"And [Eve] did eat and gave also unto her husband, with her and he did eat" (Gen. 3:6)

There are a lot of people who think that Eve was responsible for the fall. They both were punished, and some people would argue that Eve should have been singularly punished. However, it was Adam who let Eve answer the door that let evil into his home, therefore, he allowed evil into his home. He allowed a serpent into his home. A man should never allow another source to corrupt the sanctity of his home. Adam should have kicked the serpent out before he was even able to utter a single word.

God created man, and Adam had to be the perfect culmination of all of the beauty that exists in the world; sunsets, fields of orchids, breathtaking mountain views, serene horizons; everything that is spectacular in the world, was put together to create this striking man, who surely had overwhelming physical traits, and Eve, she had to be something out of this world.

One of my favorite songs is the Commodores, "Brick House". Eve had to have been a "brick house." She had to be the true definition of flawless beauty. When she opened the door and let Lucifer in, I can imagine that he was no beastly character. I can imagine that music came pouring in with every step he took into their home, heavenly music. Lucifer was supposed to be one of the most handsome angels in heaven. He was a warrior, an archangel, so Adam should have been taken aback by this splendor that was talking to his wife, but he wasn't. He allowed the devil to sneak in, and before either of them knew what was happening, they were being sailed further and further away from God.

I paint this picture to illustrate that temptation in our lives is masked the same way. It is cunning and beguiling, and isn't putrefying in it's packaging. We eat up every ounce of the bait that is thrown at us, and slowly lose ourselves to the allure of escape. The seed of deception is stealthy and will sneak into your heart, and before you know it is there, you have been swindled and are sailing further and further away from God. When we are caught, engulfed in the pits of temptation, we are made shameful, just like Adam and Eve, when they realized they were naked and tried to clothe themselves before God.

Do not let alcohol and drugs enter into your home. Do not let temptation's pretty disguise trick you into losing yourself and straying from God. Close the door on the serpent before he even decides to put your address into his GPS. You do this by making sure God is always present in your life. Make Him a constant in your life and believe that His words are true. He has a beautiful destiny awaiting you. You have to claim it, and keep temptation out there lost at sea.

Death waits for us all,

> but so does life.

> Choose life while

> you are still *breathing*.

My name is Teresa and I am not an addict, but the men I meet...well let's just say they have all successfully managed to make me apart of their addiction. I married very young. I often use to think about the cliché of a woman marrying a man that reminded her of her father, and I thought about how far from the truth this was in my situation.

My father wasn't a drunk. My father never put his hands on me. He never threatened to kill me if I left him. As a young wife, its terrifying to think about walking away from your marriage, but even more threatening, when it is a matter of more than moral. So, I told myself that this is how a husband is supposed to love his wife. I told myself that he just loved me so much and didn't know how to express that love in positive way, but love was love.

He would go out at all hours of the night, drinking and come stumbling back home. I hated the smell of alcohol, and it would just seethe through his skin. When he would come home, he would just start beating on me for no reason. He would go on and on about himself. I guess that when he drank, it boasted his ego, or bruised it perhaps, and he would just go on and on about himself. He wouldn't even let me go to sleep. Every time I would close my eyes he would hit me, and yell, "I'm not done, yet, bitch."

Sometimes, he would sit on me and hold my eyes open with his fingers. He would just keep going on and on about himself, and this man loved me.

I had two children with this monster. When I got pregnant with my second child, I was terrified. I didn't want to have another baby with this man. I would stand at the top of the stairs thinking about falling, all the time, but I knew it wasn't right for me to take a life. My child was a blessing from God and what right did I have?

My life was a mess, but I managed to clean it up a little and get away from him. We lasted seven years and six months. Two years after our marriage ended, I thought I found real love and remarried.

My idea of love is really messed up more than I know, because my new husband loved me in the same way as my first husband. This time, we were together 23 years though. I should have known this man was a drunk and a druggie. On the night of our wedding, he said he had a gift. I thought it was something special, but he pulled out a bag of white powder. He told me it would make us both feel better.

I was so hurt, so broken. I ran out of the room and I cried. I told God I had married a man that was no better than the first one, but I wanted it to work. I wanted to fix him. I wanted to fix my cycle of lackluster love. I wanted to fix what I knew was a doomed marriage. I didn't want to fail again.

I tried my best to be a good wife. I thought that if I was good enough, he would stop drinking and doing drugs. I thought that if I was good enough, he would stop putting me down all of the time, but my best was not good enough for him. I turned cold towards him. I put my children and my job first and put my marriage on the backburner, because I knew that if I put my best effort at being the best mom and employee, I would actually get results.

I began to hate everything about him. I hated constantly having to bail him out of jail. I hated his sorry excuses. I hated everything about him, but I was terrified to leave him, but the fear came more out of fear of failing then fear of him. This was my last shot, and although I was miserable in marriage, being miserable alone was more terrifying.

One day, he got the nerve to go to rehab. What a joke that was. He was a worst sober person than he was a drunk. After a couple of failed attempts at rehab, somehow he became Mister Savior A.A. He would bring home dirty, smelling men, and he wanted me to open my house to them. When I told him that no more drunks were allowed in my house, he got really upset. He would

try and hide and get drunk. I guess A.A didn't help him after all. He began
to revert back to his old ways.

After 23 years of being with a man that I hated, I met a man that truly
loved me. I got the courage to leave and I learned that leaving didn't equal
failure, but staying did. He was my angel, my saving grace. He loved me in a way
that didn't hurt. He has given me so much happiness. I never thought that I could
find a man like this, but love is never late. Love is always right on time; and it is
about time, that I loved my life. That's all.

**Women, never let a man take you down his road to destruction.
Love should never be physical, unless it is blissful, and it should
never be painful. You are not here to fix people. We are all put here
simply to love. You have to have serenity over the things that you
can't change, while acknowledging that change is good, although
sometimes inconvenient.**

My name is Robert Bauldwin and I am an addict... I have thirty
days to day. That's all

I LOVE YOU

I think that the word *love* is used so much by those addicted to drugs and alcohol. For me, it was because it was the only good thing left inside of me. I can imagine that sentiment being true for a lot of people walking through the valley to sobriety. The problem with using the word love because of it's affirming presence, is that we often use it when we don't mean it.

Some of us fall in love right out the gate of a new relationship because we feel it is the only redeeming quality about us, so we tell complete strangers that we love them and try to do everything in our power to experience it; but the Bible says that love never fails, so your love should not be treated with the regard of a trial and error, or an experiment. You should fully open your heart to love because love stands forever. If, when you are using the word, you realize you are not using it in it's totality, encompassing the exactness of forever, then don't use it.

I recently had a moment of mental clarity when I sat and thought about the power in knowing that God is love. Knowing that He is all around us all the time, because love is all around us all the time, brought me closer to Him. Knowing that He is forever in me, because the good me, the love in me, is everlasting.

I am definitely more selective in who I say I love you to. You should definitely spread love when you can. Spread God when you can, but do it in a healthy way that doesn't compromise the God in you, and remember that forever is a long time. So, when you look at a person and realize you probably will get tired of them after a few months, wait to use those precious words. It will mean so much more when it comes from inside, and isn't simply a reaction to exterior facades.

*We should live
soberly,
righteously, and
Godly in this
present world.*

MY NAME IS MARY BETH AND I AM THE MOTHER OF A CHILD WHO BECAME AN ADDICT. I don't know how or why my child started using. I never used or drank, and no one that I ever dated used drugs or abused alcohol. My child meant the world to me. I would have given my life for my child. One day, the police came to my home and told me that my child, my precious little baby boy, was dead.

They said marijuana and alcohol played a factor in a fatal car crash that left my son's car wrapped around a tree. They told me how sorry they were for my loss. I didn't know how much my heart could hurt. I felt the pain of a thousand needles pulsating in my heart, and I was so angry with God. Why would He take my child away from me, why? What had I done to deserve this? It is unnatural for a parent to outlive their children. Why me, what did I do that was so wrong?

Maybe it was my fault. As a parent, you are supposed to know certain things about your children. I should have known my son was an addict. I should have known he had a problem, and I should have been there for him. There is such an indescribable pain you feel when your child dies. I felt that I didn't want to live anymore. What did I have to live for? I asked God for forgiveness, because I knew I couldn't live with the pain. I just couldn't, I knew I wasn't strong enough. I closed my eyes, and when I opened them my child was standing there in front of me, more beautiful than I could ever remember him. He was perfect. He told me that he was always going to be with me. He told me he was sorry to make me hurt, but that he loved me very much. I got to tell him that I loved him one last time. I'm glad to be here today. I had to *go through* to *get to*, and I am so thankful to God for saving me. That's all.

EVERY MOMENT IS A GIFT FROM GOD,

SO TAKE YOUR PRECIOUS

TIME

UNWRAPPING IT.

Hello, My name is Tiffany and I am the child of an addict...I think about PTSD (post traumatic stress disorder) and how I fed those feelings and how it affects my life every single day. The nightmares that I have are never ending, and I feel even more terror because of how real the nightmares feel. It is so painful and horrific to relive the past...the hunger. I remember vividly, feeding my brothers and sisters scraps and not eating myself. It is never easy, forcing yourself to be content with an empty stomach. It is not easy having my father ask me if the night before he had been inappropriate with me. He never touched me inappropriately, but it was so devastating for him to have to ask. Those memories have sort of seared my soul. Crack had such a powerful hold on my father and most of the time he wasn't even in control.

With my dad powerless to crack, who was I supposed to look up to? Who was supposed to protect me from harm? Who was I supposed to trust? How was I ever supposed to learn how to love, when all elements of love around me were so flawed?

I turned to my grandmother, who we all called Nana. I formed an especially tight bond with her, and though she died of cancer, our bond was so strong that not even death could break it. Nana would always tell me to pray about it and let it go to God. She told me that when the time was right, God would handle it.

Nana taught me how to be immune to the agonies of life, by loving unconditionally. She was my angel and still continues to be. I saw her struggle with addictions that were not hers and the courage she had was remarkable, truly remarkable. She remained steadfast and unwavering when the storms of life destroyed her family and completely devastated everything around her. She always had faith in God and hope for the future.

I feel grateful that life guided me closer to Nana. I am grateful for the wisdom she shared with me about life. I think about the time I tried to take my own life, all the while she was fighting for hers, and how selfish I was. She was brave enough to fight for her life, although, everything around her was falling apart. She had multiple children strung out on drugs; and yet, she still tried to fight.

My attempt to want to silence the pain by taking my own life left me with guilt, because I saw how hard she was fighting. I saw how my brothers and sisters were fighting. My Nana gave me some of her fight when I hit rock bottom, and I now value the life that God has given me and no matter how bad things get, I will continue to fight, just as my Nana fought because I know all I have to do is pray and let it go to God, and in due time, whatever the affliction is, I know that He will handle it. Thank you Nana. I look forward to talking to you in my dreams tonight. That's all.

Have you thanked God lately for your recovery?

MY NAME IS ROBERT BAULDWIN AND I AM AN ADDICT... I was talking to my wife the other night, and she asked me not to hate her because her life, our life, was out of balance. She explained how she felt that her life was up in the air, and she just didn't know what to do anymore. I know sometimes that it feels like we are going to war with the air, and although it is not such a threatening entity, we seem powerless against. However, if we simplified the fight and looked at the battles for what they really are, we realize that we are more powerful and menacing against an invisible opponent.

Yes, times are hard. Yes, we struggle to make ends meet, but we are healthy, we are surrounded by love and most importantly, we are sober. God is on our side, so what opponent stands a chance against us. That's all.

Become addicted to recovery

SAVE YOUR SORRIES

Addicts favor emotions. This is how we get back into the house, back into the grace of our families, back into the hearts of the ones we have hurt, with an emotion. At the rehab center, we are taught to show our love with deeds and actions. We are enabled to show our love without saying those simple three words. It is important for you to hear this again...and again.

> 8Whom having not seen, ye love;
> in whom, though now ye see him
> not, yet believing, ye rejoice with
> joy unspeakable and full of glory.
> **(Peter 1:8)**

Encourage a quality of mind and spirit that enables you the power to face danger and fear. Encourage a heart that loves out of purity and not selfishness. Love nowadays is so watered down. It's like coffee, it starts black and then you had sugar and cream and sometimes some syrup to flavor it; hazelnut or almond. Then you add whipped cream on top. It becomes something completely different than what it started out to be. It used to be coffee and now it's a cappuccino.

Us addicts like to overuse the word *love*. We like to tell everyone that we meet that we love them, and I think it is because we believe it is the only thing we have left in us that is good. But it is not good when it is not pure. We misuse the word to manipulate our way back into the good grace of the ones we love. We say to our children that we love them, we do the same with our parents, our grandparents, our spouses, and our friends; then we take from them, we steal, we beg, we borrow, and beguile. We had sour cream, bitters, and spices and now our coffee is something completely different. It doesn't taste good.

My name is Robert and I am an addict. I'll say it again,

I wish that all rehabs had a sign above the door that we all had to read on the way in, that stated that we were not allowed to use the phrases "I love you" or "I am sorry".

In recovery, we will learn the true meanings of these phrases, but they are so badly jaded in our addicted lives that we hardly recognize it once it is put in the cup in front of us.

Love is deeds and actions. When you walk into a room, you can feel the aroma of love in the air. No words have to be uttered. It is good to tell your wife that she is beautiful, to tell your kids that you are proud of them. That is love from the heart.

I remember when I would get stuck in the crack house; I mean, I would be there for days. At least that is what it would feel like in my mind, when in reality it would only be a day. All my money was gone. I had paid no bills, and I was afraid to go home; a grown man afraid to go home. When I would return home I would abuse those favored phrases and plead my love and apologies to my family. I truly am sorry that I abused those phrases, and now perhaps, you have a hard time understanding them when they are pure, because those three words would mean something completely different when I came home, ashamed, and you went to sleep hungry. That's all.

WE CAN NO LONGER

ACT ON EMOTIONS,

WITHOUT THE BENEFIT OF THE INTELLECT.

Think before you act.

My name is Paris Bauldwin and I am the child of an addict... We had a computer once, when I was younger. It was the first computer I could remember us having. I remember being so excited about this computer. There weren't many games on it, and I was still in elementary school, so I didn't have much use for it; but we had a computer. For a poor family it meant things were looking up.

My younger brother and I came home one day and found my father hiding in his bedroom. The computer was gone, the VCR was gone and the picture of Malcolm X that once hung in the living room was gone. My dad told me to call the police and tell them that we had been robbed. I took my little brother upstairs and prayed that the police wouldn't come. I prayed my father hadn't already called them.

What would I tell the police when they asked if we saw who stole our computer? I knew who the assailant was. It was my father. He smoked our computer, and yet again, things weren't so optimistic anymore.

The hardest part about keeping the skeletons hiding in our house, was painting the picture of bliss optimism once we got to school. The forced smiles, the enthusiastic answers...we were all the perfect students. No one knew about the tear filled, sleepless nights we had, as we waited to see if our father would come home. No one knew about the belligerent tirades my father would sometimes burst into.

I remember one time my father was so out of it that he threatened to kill our dog. I had to get up and go to school the next morning, walking through the broken glass that was all over the floor, thinking in the night, my father had killed our dog. That's all I have.

EPHESIANS 5:18

Be not drunk with wine wherein excess, but be filled with the spirit.

HI MY NAME IS ROBERT AND I AM AN ALCOHOLIC... Now that I am sober, I see that there are so many different kinds of love; a love of God, a love of Jesus, a love of wife, a love of family, and a wonderfully, powerful love of self. Each one of those loves is expressed differently, making them innately different, however, they all hold the same value, and this is the truth. That's all I have.

Thank you God for your continuing grace.

(1 CORINTHIANS 1:25- 28)

25For the foolishness of God is wiser than man's wisdom, and the weakness of God is stronger than man's strength. 26Brothers, think of what you were when you were called. Not many of you were wise by human standards; not many were influential; not many were of noble birth. 27But God chose the foolish things of the world to shame the wise; God chose the weak things of the world to shame the strong. 28He chose the lowly things of this world and the despised things—and the things that are not—to nullify the things that are

MY NAME IS ROBERT BAULDWIN AND I AM AN ADDICT...I have sixty days today. I was thinking about some of the things I used to do when the crack was gone, and I had nowhere to go. How I used to sleep on other people's porches or in the back of people's pick up trucks, hoping that they wouldn't wake up before I woke up. Sometimes I would even sleep in the woods on the hard terrain and most of the time it was unbearably cold. Now that I am sober, things are quite different. I sleep in a bed now. That's all.

In order not to let the past bother you, you have to go back into the valley and stare at the shadows. Once you have figured out what lives in those shadows you become better equipped to face sobriety.

Breathe in the spirit of God.

MY NAME IS PARIS BAULDWIN AND I AM THE CHILD OF AN ADDICT...Love is one thing that has always been somewhat foreign to me. I know what it is, and I know how it feels to be loved, but it wasn't until I opened my heart to God that I fully understood it.

Love is how God is expressed throughout humanity. I got a tattoo recently. I know my dad is going to kill me after he reads this, but it says, "God is Love" in Arabic. I believe that wholeheartedly. He isn't some big heavenly being that sits on a throne in the clouds looking down at us humans, amused by our missteps. God is the love we express to our children and neighbors. God is the love we express to our siblings and family members, as well as the love we express to perfect strangers.

People always ask me why I am so upbeat and positive most of the time, my response is that it is the God in me, the love in me. I could have turned all of my past fragments of hurt and pain into more pain and hurt, but God entered my heart and his presence there is something so powerful that even on my bad days, I find solace in doing good for others by expressing my love for them.

Now I am far from perfect, I can't find love for EVERYONE, especially because I live in Los Angeles, and just yesterday I was tempted to cuss out the man who cut me off on the freeway, but I try my best to interact with EVERYONE with love and humility; because, after all, HE saved me. Therefore, it is my position to be God like, not perfect, that would be a disappointment, but God like, so that I can continue to reap the fruits of His word. So I am learning to speak the language of love that was once as foreign as Arabic to me. That's all.

Sometimes I feel like using but I don't feel like being used. Stay sober.

IT'S OKAY TO...

THE TEARS, THEY FALL AS IF THEY ARE THE DEFINITION OF GRAVITY

THE PAIN, I WISH IT WOULD STAY...WITH BREVITY

BUT IT STAYS, AS A CHRONIC REMINDER

OF WHAT I DID TO ME.

Sometimes, out of nowhere, we just want to cry for no reason. We don't want people to see us cry, because we are not doing it for sympathy or for show. We simply feel like crying. Sometimes it can be bad, but mostly it's good. Cry when you feel good; when you are in a moment that seems like a dream, but it's your sober reality. Cry when you thank God for saving you. Cry when you hear your kids say they love you and are proud of you. Cry when you want your heart to feel free. Cry, so when you have to cry through your tribulations your tears will evoke a memory of happiness and not pain.

MY NAME IS JOY AND I AM AN ADDICT...I have seven days sober, and each day gets harder than the day before. I cry almost every night. I never used to cry when I used drugs. It is something so strange to me...this feeling of feeling again. It has been so long since I cried, and I don't know if that is good or bad. I know after I cry, I feel better. Then it feels bad, because I think about all of the inhumane things I did in my addiction.

I feel so full of shame, when I think about the things I did to get drugs...the number of men I slept with. When I was a little girl, I wanted to keep myself away from boys, because I wanted to save myself for one man, and that man would be my husband. That dream ended when my mother's brother, my uncle, raped me when I was fourteen. Of course my mother didn't believe me, and when I tried to tell her I had been a virgin up until the incident, she just walked away from me. From that day, I looked at men as animals and those animals meant nothing to me. Just get it over with and give me the crack.

I cry so much now, because I want God in my life. I need a man to take care of me, and I desperately want that man to be God. Please, God be that man that makes me feel alive again. I want to have a relationship with you, but I don't know how to be loved or how to love. God, please teach me how to love. I never felt it before in my life. I've never been touched by love.

Every day of sobriety, I find myself liking myself more. I try to be better, each day, than I was the day before. I believe that God answers prayers and the more that I wash myself in His words, then the closer I get to Him. I don't think about drugs as much as I used to because I have fallen in love for the first time in my life. Thank you God. That's all.

GOD HAS CHOSEN YOU TO DO GOOD THINGS IN YOUR RECOVERY.

DO THEM.

THAT'S GOD'S WILL.

YES YOU HAVE DONE SOME BAD THINGS IN YOUR LIFE.

DO THE GOOD THINGS NOW

*My name is Erin and I am an addict...*I understand.

I feel. I want. I understand that I am playing with fire. I feel that I am confused. I want to overcome an addiction. These are words that can keep one grounded, especially someone trying to overcome an addiction. That's all.

My name is Julia and I am an addict. My drug of choice was ice, crystal meth. Sitting here, so many thoughts are running through my head; of course I am high and I have not slept in 3 ½ days. I have no more money to continue my habit, and I am at my breaking point. It is now or never. I have to hit the brakes or continue to go down this path of pure self-destruction. I see myself losing things like my car, my self-esteem, my money and most importantly my mind. How do I get back on track, especially if a big part of me doesn't want to stop? I love ice...like I used to love myself. Pitiful, huh?

I am living a life of constant isolation. It is more comfortable to push those around me away, unless they wished me harm. I have become mildly OCD. I am constantly counting, washing my hands, and then straightening up the kitchen. I see myself deteriorating, but I cannot do anything about it.

I started hearing voices recently. I knew they weren't there, but I started answering them back anyway. I completely silenced God. I lost touch with Him, because I thought that He had left me. That was, after all, why I was forced to hurt so much. I know it is silly, because I know, that in times when we hear Him the least, we are actually supposed to trust Him the most. He wants us to trust in Him and get lost in Him even more when we feel that disconnect.

I am constantly searching for reasons to continue my habit; for instance, I am not hurting anyone, I pay for it myself, my children are not neglected...so many, many lies. I actually tell myself that ice is helping me. I convince myself that it helps bring out my creative side. It keeps my mind off of the everyday problems I face. It keeps me from sleeping, which keeps me from dreaming, because I hate dreaming and I hate nightmares. I've had a lot of nightmares. They say it is from PTSD. When I hit the pipe I feel relieved. It's sad, but I feel comforted and safe...elated. I can describe it as being in my own bubble. When I am here, no one else matters.

I was once addicted to horoscopes and tarot cards and things of that nature...things not of God, because I wanted to know where my life was going. Us addicts truly have addictive personalities over ever malice in our life. Although we are not in control, we want to control. This addictive personality is pulling me further and further away from Christ and my salvation. But, sitting here alone, something is whispering to me that I am worthy, and no it is not the voices I told you about. I think it is Christ trying to break through to me.

How did I get so lost? Was it when I was raped by my mom's ex boyfriend who had been welcomed into our family as a friend? Was it when the pressures of being a single mom mounted and became terrifying?

Pray...I have to pray. I've always prayed when things were too big for me to handle. And right now this is too big for me. I am overcome with great trouble and sorrow, so Lord I call out to you. I know that you protect over the simple hearted. I know **YOU** will catch me in mid air, cause I know I am falling. I accept what I have to do. I am tired, but I am ready to take back my life, my car, my self-esteem, my money, and most importantly my mind. I want to claim my salvation. That's all.

RECOVERY IS AN INSIDE JOB.

Love is the quality of imagination and individuality expressed in one's actions.

MY NAME IS ROBERT BAULDWIN AND I AM AN ADDICT...

Today I have ninety days. One of the hardest things to do is to stop thinking about using. The first months were the hardest but I learned how to transition my thoughts on using so now I think about using all the time. I think about all of the people I hurt when I was using and why I should be sober. But sometimes it's hard to keep those thoughts at the forefront. Sometimes when I think about using, I think that I should die a drunk. I have done some terrible things. I'm trying to figure this all out. I don't know how to like myself sometimes. That's all.

*

Dear addict,

Before you relapse back into your old ways...before you do that, I want you to close your eyes and imagine the repulsive, piggish, polluted and paranoid way you used to live. You were always thinking that someone was out to get you. You were constantly looking over your shoulder, afraid of your own shadow.

Imagine now, the tears in your children's eyes, as their little hearts were being shattered. Imagine how afraid they are, how unstable and insecure they are, because they don't know if mom or dad will protect them. They are all alone, and they cannot run and hide anywhere. There is nowhere to go. Just imagine it. Now open your eyes.

Stay sober for them. They need you.

THIS LITTLE LIGHT OF MINE

The darkness never wants light to shine, because it has the power of destroying the lie. Kept in the cave of obscurity, never exposed by the light, the lie lives, and gains its power. The power it has to confine and enslave ones mind grows stealthily, making sobriety impossible.

Don't put out the light inside. It is the spirit of God. Let His star shine in your heart. Accept Him fully into your heart and let Him light up the path to sober living. Let him light up the path to recovery for you. You have to be willing to give Him everything in order for that light to shine. He wants it all. Give it to Him. It is that simple.

In the Bible, it says, "watch and be sober." Now Paul is not talking about being drunk, solely. Being sober has many different forms. Being sober involves not becoming intoxicated with this world and not being conformed. You are children of the day, meaning children of the light. Even at night you still walk with the light. Don't ever forget that. Don't ever let the lie win.

There was a commercial I saw on TV that says, "You are in good hands". It was about car insurance, but just apply that to Jesus. You are in good hands with Jesus. When you leave your home, Jesus wants you to have sobriety, to be unaffected by the disillusions of this world. He wants you to look **fear** and tribulation in the face and run full speed towards the bright horizon he has planned for you. You are the children of the **light**. Keep that light with you always. Keep His light with you always.

There was a man on the side of the road, and when Jesus passed by, he cried out for Him. People nearby, told him to be quiet; but he cried out even louder.

Jesus turned and asked how could he help the man. The man explained to Jesus that he was blind and wanted desperately to see.

Jesus healed the man and told him that it was his faith that made him well. Just think, if the man wouldn't have cried out and just listened to the darkness, he would still be blindly wondering on that road.

If we become

successful in not using we

will achieve and fulfill our goals

in life: to have peace on earth and a heavenly state of mind.

(1 *PETER* 3:17)

For it is better, if
the will of God be
so, that ye suffer
for well doing than
for evil doing.

An addict is like a wave of the sea, tossed and driven

by the winds. He is unstable in every way.

Recovery is when you wake up and know you did the right thing yesterday.

My name is Rena and I am an addict... Today, I have two years sober. I have this glorious opportunity to be present; present in the heart of my mom and dad, present in the life of my big brother, and present in my own life. I want to thank God for loving me all the way back to my old self. I want to thank Jesus for forgiving me of my sins.

In rehab, I read the Bible more times than I had ever read it in my entire life. In the book of Peter, it says that it is better if we suffer for well doing for the will of God than for evil doing.

When I first left home for school, I got my Bachelors. Then I went back to go all the way: to get my PhD in accounting. I started my own accounting business, and for the first year, I worked very hard. The hard worked paid off. I was able to employ five other people to work for me. One of the employees, Tim, asked me one day, how long it had been since the last time I went out, let my hair down and had a little fun. I replied with the cliché, "I don't have time for that kind of stuff."

Tim was very insistent on me letting my hair down, so one day he introduced me to his cousin. I hadn't been on a date, ever really...I mean, I had been with men, just not dated them, if you get my drift. Anyways, Tim's cousin was this tall, good-looking man, and he caused my imagination to freely roam.

I thought about being happy and complete with someone, and this man certainly satisfied a great percentage of what I desired. However, my free running imagination is the root of where things went wrong. Tim's cousins name was Frank. We hit it off very well.

We began having a sexual relationship. To be honest, it just felt good to have someone beside me at night. It didn't even bother me when I found out Frank was married.

One day, when Frank was getting dressed and about to leave my place, something fell from his pants pocket. I became angry when I realized that it was drugs, but he insisted that it was nothing major and that I needed to quit being so judgmental, because I might like it if I tried it.

So, there I was, half dressed, in my bed, with a married man who pours out a line of coke on my table; like what they do in the movies. He began snorting it. Who was I to judge, as I was there, with a half naked married man? I couldn't resist it when he offered it to me.

I sniffed it and inhaled it. I felt a way I had never felt in my life. It was such an intense feeling, like I had my first orgasm, but it was far better than any kind of sex. It felt so good, that I thought to myself, why did I need a man? The essence of what I wanted was right in front of me. I felt, in my heart, that if there was something in this world that made me feel this great, it had to be no good for me.

I felt the same about Frank, and my resentment for him grew, until I told him I had had enough. He acted surprised like living this adulterous life was normal. I told him I didn't want to do it anymore and that he should go home to his wife. He pulled his fist back and with all the power in him, struck me so hard that my feet came out from beneath me. As I as struggling to come to, he injected me with something and climbed on top of me and had sex with me.

The drugs in my system magnified the feeling of everything. I was angry with myself for finding such immense gratification in what was going on. The way the drugs made me feel was remarkable. All I could remember, when he was finished, was being unable to move. I lied there on the floor for an entire day. When I finally came to, I realized that I had missed work. I called in to check on things. Tim answered the phone, and I could hear Frank in the background. He had to have been telling Tim all the sordid details; so, ashamed, I told Tim to keep Frank there, and I got dressed and headed to work. Of course Frank was gone by the time I made it there. I was so angry and full of shame that I told Tim to pack his things and go find another job.

I asked Jean, one of the ladies in the office, to run things for a while. I went back home to find that Frank had let himself into my home. I asked the doorman to escort me upstairs so that he could escort Frank out.

When we walked into my home, Frank was sitting on my sofa. He looked really desperate and told me he needed some money. I asked the doorman to step out and Frank explained to me how much he loved me and how much he knew I loved him. I knew in my heart that this was complete bull and I wanted him to leave. Then, he put some drugs on the table.

I was instantly recalled to that moment of immense satisfaction, and against my better judgment, I got high with Frank. I am not certain when the doorman returned to his post and left, but once it was all gone, Frank told me he needed some money to go and score us some more drugs. I gave him my ATM card, again, against my better judgment.

Two days later the bank called and said I had been spending money very rapidly, and it caused them to be alarmed. They said I had spent over $50,000 in a period of 24 hours. I had them cancel the card. I curled up on my sofa and examined how this tsunami had completely destroyed my life in such a short amount of time.

A week into my depression, I hear a knock at my door, thinking it was Frank I didn't move. The knock would not go away, so I answered it, prepared to yell at the person on the other side; to my surprise it was my brother. He had been trying to reach me and was checking up on me to see how I was. I cried like a little baby in his arms, so ashamed of myself. I figured, since I had only had a taste, it was going to be an easy road to recovery. Let's just say, there is no such thing. I am so thankful, however, for this journey.

I am thankful for my precious gift of presence; my presence in my life, my presence in my family life and my presence in this beautiful sober life. That's all.

Absence from drugs is recovery.

My name is Robert Bauldwin and I am an addict. I have been sober for a year now and last night I was thinking about my children and how God has watched over them. I am so thankful to God for that. I wasn't a good father. I would tell my children that I loved them and then I would go and get high. That was not love. Love is when I don't have to say it. It is when I show it. That's real love, and I thank God for that understanding. That's all.

Never let the sense of failure corrupt your new action.

THE TRUTH SHALL...

I heard someone say that the truth shall set you free. I figure, either that person knew the truth and just couldn't catch up with freedom or they caught freedom and knew nothing about the truth; because the truth is, to have truth and freedom in the same room is, quite frankly, impossible.

You may be able to start healing your soul by expressing the truth, not only to the people that you hurt, but also yourself. However, freedom will be a distant reward. Freedom comes from much more than divulging the truth. Usually, the outcome of revealing the truth is pain and suffering and acknowledgment of hurt. That hardly equates to freedom.

The person speaking the truth does, however, hold the power to allow the person hearing it the freedom to forgive them. Grant someone the freedom to forgive and start healing your soul. Let go of the notion that by telling the truth you will automatically be free, because in your attempt to be set free by your truths, you may lose both.

*My name is Robert Bauldwin and I am an addict...*One thing I hate more than anything in the world, is that I was not able to complete fatherhood because of drugs. I know God has already forgiven me for that sin, but I hope that my children can forgive me, as well.

Fatherhood is something to be cherished. It is a gift from God. I missed out on that. I have beautiful children who had a ghost of a father, and I just pray they have forgiven me.

Love your family. Trust me, it will keep you sober.

*Hello my name is Erin and I am an addicted child of an addict...*I talked to my mother recently, and she laid everything out on the table. Our conversation brought me a step closer to this beautiful evolution that is getting ready to take place in my life. It is overwhelming. I am feeling anxious, unsure, vulnerable, peaceful, faithful and hopeful all at once. God answers prayers. He is always on time and like a faithful servant I will wait for Him. Thank you Jesus. I completed my treatment today, and I pray that I will stay sober by the grace of God.

I am learning to love myself again. I stay grounded through the Holy Spirit. I continue to watch as God works miracles in my life.

Miracle number one: sobriety.

Miracle number two: I am working full time at a job that makes me feel good.

Miracle number three: This beautiful, God-fearing man that keeps my head on straight and loves every flaw that I have in the perfect way that God loves them.

Miracle number five: The opportunity to share my testimony. I am a survivor. I will constantly praise His name and share my story of triumph. The devil thought he had me…silly, silly devil.

I read this affirmation daily:

I am a child of God

I am made in God's liking

I am worthy

In Him all things are possible

Thank YOU for blessing me, regardless of my faults

Please keep me on the path of righteousness

I want to do YOUR will

I am grateful….Thank You, Lord

Today I am sober…

I talk BIG, ACT BIG, and look like SUCCESS

I will proceed with confidence. That's all.

Dear Addict,

" Be sober. Be vigilant, because your adversary, the devil, as a roaring lion, walketh about seeking whom he may devour" (1 PETER 5:8)

So stay sober, so as not to blind your sights of the approaching enemy.

My name is Michael and I am an addict...I have one year of sobriety. I used to tell myself that I would never be like my father. Most of us who say that end up like me, becoming the mirror image of the thing we hated.

My father died at the age of 46. He was very young. He drank so much that it destroyed his liver. We never had a really good father-son relationship, and the times we did bond, it wasn't genuine, because he was too drunk to remember. Most of the memories I have of my father are of him drunk. That's not good. I wish my father would have played with me...at least without being drunk. I wish he would have told me that he loved me. I wish he would have hugged me when he was sober.

I believe this gene was past down by his family. I don't believe it was by heredity. I believe that it was a learned behavior. Today, I know I don't HAVE to be like my earthly father. Even though his blood flows through my body, and I look a lot like him, I don't have to be like him, and yes, I have forgiven him. I guess he did the best he could. I never went without anything. I had food to eat and a roof over my head, so I guess he did the best he could. However, I have a new father now. He tells me He will be with me all of the time. He has and will continue to provide for me. That's all.

My name is Robert Bauldwin and I am an addict... When we make amends to someone, it is best received if we cut out the overly emotional parts and just ask for forgiveness. All the other, overly sentimental, crap will fall on deaf ears. Don't push too much on the person you are seeking forgiveness from. You will push them away.

Jesus was the savior of our world. He was our bridge over troubled waters. He asked for those who were crucifying Him to be forgiven, because they knew not what they were doing. His death gave us a way back into the kingdom of heaven. As long as Jesus was alive, we had no hope. He had to die for us to live.

If Satan would have known that, he would have found a way for Jesus to die from old age. We know now that through his death we were given liberation to live. In living, we have to understand how He was strong enough to ask God to forgive us. It takes an unimaginable strength, to hang from a cross, bloodied and beaten, and find serenity to ask for forgiveness for your trespassers.

Be strong and ask those who you have trespassed against for forgiveness, and, also be open to giving forgiveness, too. Hurt people, hurt people. Think about that and ask for forgiveness. That's all.

Forgiveness makes fear go

away,

because it creates love, which has no fear.

My name is Mary and I am an addict... I have seven days today.

Trust me when I tell you that these have been the longest seven days of my life. There were times I didn't think that I could make it, but I did. I told myself that I could do another day, just one more day. That's all.

So, if there is no Jesus, there is no forgiveness, and if there is no forgiveness, why attend A.A?

THE PROMISE KEEPER

God told Moses to go to the Promised Land, and they were excited. They thought since God sent them on this journey, that it would be an easy road. However, we all know that the journey was anything but easy. It was rough and filled with obstacles that often tested Moses's faith and understanding. However, Moses stood firm in his faith. Once they arrived at the Promised Land, they saw that it was already occupied; they knew they would have to fight to receive the promise.

In recovery we have to fight to receive all that is promised to us. We have to fight to stay sober. We have to fight to gain back our families trust. We have to fight to forgive ourselves. Just know that you have been forgiven for your addiction. Use forgiveness as your weapon to fight. Fight for your promise. When you pray, God is faithful. What you ask for, you will receive. Mark 21:22 reaffirms that for us.

"Whatsoever ye shall ask in prayer, believing ye shall receive."

My name is Paris and I am the daughter of an addict...When I think about life and how remarkable and wretched it can be, I think about how the devil seemed to have specifically targeted my family; I mean he sent out an entire arsenal to destroy and conquer. The majority of my life has been spent awaiting bad news. It is a terrible way to go through life, waiting for bad things to happen, but it seemed inevitable. Anytime I received good news, I couldn't fully celebrate, because I anticipated for it to be coupled with tragic news, because that seemed to be the blueprint of my life.

Most of my good days ended in rain, and whenever it would rain, it would hail, and thunderstorm, and hurricane and everything else. Whenever something good occurred, I held my breath just waiting for catastrophe to occur. However, I realized one day that through the spectacular down pours, I had learned so much about life, and my wisdom garnered more beauty than a double rainbow. Appreciating the pain, made the precious moments so much more splendid.

Worrying now seems so trivial because my armor was being prepared all along. I was given tests, some of which were physical and mental, but a lot of them were spiritual. These tests prepared me to be the woman that God is using to carry out His will. He has done some tremendously spectacular things for me in my life, and I know had I not been preparing through the storms, I would not be prepared for the glory that awaits me.

I am so glad that my faith has withstood after all the calamity. I am so glad that God chose me to go down this road. I enjoy rainy days, sometimes more than sunny days, depending on my mood. I am so grateful for my discernment about what's really worth crying over and what tribulations can be celebrated as blessings. Please continue to use me. That's all.

Hebrews 11:1

Faith is the

substance of things hoped for,

the evidence of things

not seen.

It is the little things that make you feel good to be sober.....the little things like saying thanks and hearing your child laugh.

My name is Robert Bauldwin and I am an addict...Today I wanted to use so badly that my body hurt. I got through it with God. I didn't use. That's all

I love my wife with all of my heart, but I love God way more. She is ok with that.

LOST AND FOUND

Every decision we make has consequences, both good and bad. Today, you have made the good and upright decision of staying sober. God loved us so much that He gave us free will and the right to choose. We get to choose whether we love Him or not. That is powerful. We, also, have the power to choose whether to smoke crack or not, to go out and drink or stay home with our families, to shoot up or not, or to love whole heartedly the ones that love us in the perfect nature of God's love.

You have the power to walk away from your vices and love God in your recovery. The best thing about this, though, is God is going to love you regardless of what choices you make. If you find yourself in the midst of a bad decision, God's perfect love will help guide you back to where you need to be. That's powerful.

I pray that God will bless you in your recovery; that you may redeem some of the things you have lost along the way. I am not speaking about material things. I am talking about things that matter to the heart, things that will leave an impression on the soul. This is something you cannot see. These things are like faith.

We must cut the umbilical cord of our addictive life.

Disconnect and live on your own.

MY NAME IS ROBERT BAULDWIN AND I AM AN ADDICT...I was at a meeting the other night, and I heard this guy say that when he first stopped using, his sponsor told him to forget about anything that he had ever known. That advice sounded a little crazy to me. It was like a doctor prescribing putting a patient into a coma, so that he, or she, could heal from their affliction without feeling any pain.

Part of the healing process is understanding and enduring the pain. You have to fully understand how your actions have caused pain, not only in your life, but in the lives of others. Exploring that pain is the remedy. Knowing how to deal with those feelings without turning to drugs and alcohol is the remedy, not locking them up in a closet, because eventually that closet will become full and all those dark memories will overcome you like a flash flood.

You can not simply forget your past, especially when every time you come to a meeting, you revisit it. If we all attempted to live by the notion of forgetting, we would come to these meetings and sit and silence, not really knowing how to help one another. We wouldn't be able to share our stories of resilience through the dark valleys. I encourage you to remember your past, so you won't repeat it again. Never go dumb and forget everything, because everything you go through in life both good and bad is purposed to prepare you for what's ahead. That's all.

Work hard to make sure you never go back to using drugs.

THERE ONCE WAS A MAN... who on pay day would mail cash his check, get a $50 money order and then mail it to himself, that way when he spent all of his money on crack, the money order would come in the mail just in time to buy one last hit.

(ACTS 9:11)

"And the Lord said unto Saul, arise and go to a street called 'Straight'."

God wanted Saul, just like he wants us, to get our lives straight. As addicts, figuring out the intricate web we have built out of our addictive lives is quite the task, but we are pushed, not only by God, but by our families and those that love us to go to a street called "Straight" and get it together.

MY NAME IS ROBERT BAULDWIN AND I AM AN ADDICT... I could never understand why a 20 year old man, who was doing well with his life, would walk into a bathroom, take a big drink of Jack, put a gun to his head, and attempt to take his own life. 30 years later, I understand why I put the gun to my head. I am so happy that it misfired, and I am so thankful to be alive. That's all.

Love is when you did okay yesterday, drug free.

THE PROMISE PATH

HOW CAN I TRUST, IF I CAN'T SEE?

HOW CAN I SEE IF I AM BLIND?

IT'S EASIER TO BASE THE FUTURE ON THE PAST

LIVING MY LIFE CONSTANTLY IN REWIND.

You are at a resting place in your life. Your present position is not a destination; it is just a stopping point in your journey. Each place you have ever visited was purposed, however, you need to use those past coordinates and map out a beautiful, bountiful future. You can change the course of your life and make sure your paths lead you in a positive direction.

Stop going round and round in the circles of misery. Stop using rehab as hideout until the first of the month when you will have the money to pay the dope dealer that fronted you drugs. Stay awhile and really listen. Make the right choices in your recovery. Take the necessary steps out of the labyrinth and onto a path lined with promise and potential.

It is okay to ask why,

because

"why" + "wait" = an answer.

Hi, my name is Rosalynn and I am an addict...When I was thirteen years old, I stopped loving life. Before then, I loved life, and I would talk to God everyday. I told God that I would wait until I was married to give myself away. Well, I started dating this boy that was five years older than me. He made me feel so special and different. The boys my age didn't make me feel the way he did.

One day, he asked me to come over to his house. I kept telling myself what I had promised God, and at first, my spirit told me not to go, but I decided to go because my flesh wanted me to. So, I went. As soon as I walked into the house, he began kissing on me and started ripping my clothes off. I begged and pleaded with him to stop, but he kept on going. Two other boys came out from a room in the back and they began raping me. They kept me there for thirteen hours, and as I lay there in my own blood, crying, I heard them laughing. They dropped me back off at home, and as I walked in, all I could do was cry.

I asked my daddy to forgive me, because I wasn't a virgin anymore. I told him about the three guys and what they had done to me. He told my mother not to call the police. He began crying and told me and my mom never to tell anyone what had happened. My daddy left. He drove around in his pick up truck until he found those three boys. He asked them if they had done those terrible things to me. They laughed and told him that I asked for it. My daddy pulled his gun out and killed those three boys. He unloaded and reloaded his gun several times.

That evening on the news, the police announced how they were looking for the gang that had done that to those boys. They blamed their death on a gang feud. I was thirteen and I hated life. Life wasn't pure, or innocent anymore. It was full of hatred and sorrow. Now, I am here, and I want to get help. I know God allows certain things to happen. I just hope that He stays with me through this. That's all.

There are some places in a man's heart that may never be known until he enters the gates of heaven.

Will you die with a pipe in our mouth? After stealing from your family to buy crack, will you die with that shame in your heart or with that bottle in your hand? Today is the day of redemption, salvation and reformation. Make the changes that are necessary today, while it is still today.

My name is Robert Bauldwin and I am an addict... On September 14, 2010, my younger brother was sent to jail. It hurt... really hurt deep down in my heart, because as siblings, we try to shelter one another. But I didn't have a drink. Thanks be to God. That's all

We are not bad people. Remember that in your sobriety.

In recovery, we must absolutely abstain from drugs and alcohol and anything that will lead us astray. We have to grow in grace in recovery.

Growing in grace will keep us from

going   astray

Where there is no vision, the people disappear, as if they never existed. When you use drugs and alcohol, you become invisible. Your vision is impaired and your imagination disappears. You simply do not exist. Regain your vision. Reclaim your life.

JOY AND GRACE

Hello, my name is Grace and I am the friend of an addict...My father is a preacher, and he said, my name would grow right inside of me. Ever since I was a little girl, he would tell me that nothing from the outside would take away my joy, because after all, my joy was God given, so how could man be powerful enough to take it away? He taught me all about the Bible and how it would protect me in times of need, whenever I was lonely or insecure, or unsure about life.

One day, we were on our way to church. I remember, it was a beautiful day outside and the sky was a magnificent blue and the sun was beaming, but not too hot, and I saw her again. There was this girl, about my age, who would just come and stand outside of the church. I was 15 at the time, and at first, I thought she was just strange, but then her mystery, really began to intrigue me. She would just stand there and watch as all of the people walked in and out of the church. She would stand and watch, expressionless; and when church was over, a man would come and put her in a car and then she would be gone, until next week.

I would hope and pray that she would be there in front of the church, because I had convinced myself every week that I would invite her inside, but every week, for whatever reason, I chickened out. One week, however, I told my father about her. I asked him if it would be okay for me to invite her as my guest. My father told me he didn't think that would be a good idea, because she might be a prostitute or something. I could tell he was half trying to protect me and half trying to protect the congregation, however, I reminded him that he once told me that Paul would do anything in hopes that he could win some for Jesus. I also reminded him of the prostitute who poured oil onto the feet of Jesus. Before I got too far ahead of myself, I remember my father cutting me off and telling me that it just wouldn't look right to have a prostitute sitting amongst his congregation in church.

I was so puzzled, because my father was the same man who told me that Jesus died in front of the church for the weak and the sick. I wanted so badly to use this opportunity to make someone strong...strong in Jesus. I argued in her favor all night long, and my father finally gave in and said that it was alright for me to invite her.

So Sunday came around and I walked over to her. She was standing in the same spot she always stood in, with her blank stare. I asked her if she would like to come inside with me, half afraid of rejection, half afraid she'd turn and run away. To my surprise she said yes. As we began to walk up the stairs, I asked her name. She responded in almost a whisper, saying that her name was Joy. When she said that, I looked up to the sky and smiled. God sure has a sense of humor.

Being the child of the preacher meant we got to church exceptionally early each Sunday, so there was still about an hour before service started. I took her to the bathroom in my father's study where there was a shower. I told her that she could get cleaned up before service if she liked. I had brought some clothes from home and gave them to her. I asked her age and she replied saying she was 13 or 15. She couldn't remember. I ensured her it was okay, and that I wasn't asking to judge, but simply to hear her testimony. So she shared it with me.

*

My name is Joy and I am the addicted child of an addict... When I was little, my mom took me from my daddy. My mom used to put this stuff in her arm. I saw her do it all the time. She sold me one day to the man who used to give her the stuff to put in her arm. He started giving me the same stuff he gave her, and I never saw my mommy again. I remember though, my father, who my mom took me from, saying that if I got lost to go to the church. He said he would come and get me. I come here everyday. I wait outside looking for him. But I can't never find him, and I pray to him every day....

After hearing her testimony, I wanted to find my father so that we could find her father. I marched to the front of the church where service was about to begin. Everyone was settling in their seats, and I saw my father across the room. Joy followed timidly behind me. As I approached my father, so did a man wearing all black. He stared through me to Joy; and my father saw the way the man stared. The man began to approach Joy and me. My father stopped him and he told my father that he only wanted to get what was his.

I shook my head and stood in front of Joy to protect her. My father stepped in front of me. He told the man that he couldn't let him take Joy out of the church. The man pulled out a gun and pointed it at my father, and demanded that he get out of the way. My father stood there boldly and said that if it was his time, then he was okay with that, but that the man would have to go through him to get to Joy.

The entire congregation had become engrossed at this point. Everyone was staring. A man stood and told the man that he would have to go through more than just the good preacher. Realizing he was out numbered, the man lowered his gun. He looked around at all of the people and then stared to Joy who had begun to cry. Her cry was so piercing; it shook my soul. The police came and took the man away.

I bet that no one had done anything nice for her, or stood up for her ever. We found Joy's biological father days later. When Joy was three years old, her mother kidnapped her. She had been missing for 11 years.

She and I became great friends through the years. She still struggles sometimes, but I won't loose her to this. My father always told me that no one could take my joy. That's all.

WE ALL HAVE A SEASON TO SHINE.

SOMETIMES WE DON'T RECOGNIZE THE SEASON AND OTHER TIMES WE DO.

SOMETIMES THE WIND BLOWS THEM AWAY AND SOMETIMES THEY STAY,

BUT WE ALL HAVE A SEASON, AND I PRAY,

THAT I HAVE ANOTHER SEASON IN ME.

My name is Robert and I am an addict...I will glorify God for the rest of my life, then after my life, I will continue to glorify God. You see, God saved my life from drugs and alcohol. God saved my life, when I put a gun to my head and tried to pull the trigger. It misfired. God saved my life, when I was running from the police and I jumped over a fence and fell off a cliff. I broke my leg. It took the rescue personnel four hours to get me out, but God saved my life. God also saved my life, when I was on the edge of a building, ready to die, because I thought I had nothing to live for. God saved me when I jumped from the third floor...it should have killed me, but God saved me. That's all.

Jesus is the antidote to any addiction.

COME HOME

Got paid yesterday,

All my money's gone.

No food in the fridge.

Phone and gas are off.

How can I live like this,

Knowing that it's wrong?

Got paid yesterday.

You would never know.

When an addict is out of all of his money, he prays for forgiveness. He pleads to be forgiven for all of his sins. He cries and deep down in his heart, he sincerely wants forgiveness. As he falls to his knees, begging for mercy, he is simply forgiven. It is that simple. Ask and ye shall receive. Ask and ye shall be made whole again.

However, when that addict stands back to his feet, he remembers the money he gave to his daughter to pay the light bill. He finds his daughter and takes that money back and leaves behind empty promises. He goes straight to the dope man.

We addicts are like the prodigal son. He took all of the money from his father. He spent all of his money partying every night and drinking. He spent all of his money on corrupt things to satisfy his carnal cravings. Now, I don't know what kind of drugs they had back in those days, but I know one thing, it was pure. I'm sure a large part of his money was spent to satisfy his hunger for his choice toxin. Anyway, he awoke one day and had no money left. He was living amongst pigs, just like you and I live among pigs in the crack house.

The prodigal son came to his senses, however, and realized he needed to return home, and fast. The best part of the story, however, was that upon his return home, his father was waiting for him with open arms, just like God is waiting for you and I with open arms. Why don't we just return on home?

THE THINGS I PRAY YOU REDEEM, ARE THINGS
LIKE GOD'S LOVE.

NONE OF US HAVE SEEN HIM,

YET, WE LOVE HIM WITH ALL OF OUR HEART AND SOUL.

MY NAME IS ROBERT BAULDWIN AND I AM AN ADDICT... I want to give all the glory, honor and praise to God, who loved me even when I was still in my sin. I also want to give thanks to God for giving us His son. When we first come to the A.A meetings, we want to be liked. As strange as that sounds, it is true; and there is nothing wrong with wanting to be liked. It is important, on this journey to find your true sober self, that you don't get lost or blinded.

Just like every diamond has its flaw, the Bible has its flaws and the A.A book has its flaws, therefore, it is important to stay true to the good person that is inside of you.

In my journey to sobriety, I have heard mention of being recovered from alcoholism, however, it has been my experience that everything that I did to my family and to myself came from making choices...bad choices. I can't say that I was sick with any affliction, but I just got caught in making a series of bad choices due to my addiction. The founder of A.A claims to have been healed from a medical disorder, however, I beg to differ that he just decided to make a choice to start living right, as I encourage you to do. I did and for the first time, I am breathing and living. It is an amazing feeling. I am thankful to God for saving me, not healing, but saving me. That's all.

Do something good for yourself and love who you are.

Before we were formed in our mother's womb we walked with God and played with God in our thoughts, then He spoke is into existence. We need to walk with God again. That's recovery. Walking with God. Let's all take our first steps again; our first steps back in the presence of God.

WORK HARD

In order to stay sober you must work hard at it. You must appreciate a new way of life to be able to recognize the quality and significance of your choice to stay sober. It is a magnificent, valuable accomplishment, because you did it for *yourself*.

In working hard, however, we all will fall short of the glory of God. Nonetheless, there comes a time, that we must stop falling for drugs. When you stop using drugs, after a long period of time, you will have dreams so bad that it will make you not want to sleep. The nightmares, slowly cease, and the beauty in dreaming becomes very precious. Stay sober.

TALK SOFT

In recovery, we must change our communication skills; the way we talk to people. The language we used in the crack house or the words spoken in inebriation were degrading, not only to the person who heard them, but also to ourselves. We spoke to our loved ones with humiliating language, often times, because we did not know how to articulate what was truly on our minds. We made a pattern out of poor articulation; however, in recovery we have to counter that habit and create a habit of expressing our feelings and thoughts adequately without defiling who we are.

In the A.A book, it talks about a psyche change involving the soul and the spirit forging and becoming one. Reestablish and reform the way you think, feel and behave. This will ultimately change the way we speak, and the words we speak will become easier to hear. Our loved ones will appreciate it.

(2 Timothy 2:15)

Study to shew thyself approved unto God, a workman that needeth not to be ashamed, rightly dividing the word of truth.

First of all, I would like to thank God for His compassion, His love and His amazing grace.

MY NAME IS ROBERT BAULDWIN AND I AM AN ADDICT. I want to thank Him for allowing me to be here. See, God saved my life, and that is why I glorify his name. No man could make me believe that I was forgiven for all of my sins, but God made me believe. He made me feel that everything bad I had done was no longer relevant to my present position in life, and this is why I am sober today. That's all.

My name is Paris Bauldwin and I am the child of an addict. We pray for people who are doing wrong. We pray for them to get better. We pray for them to get back on the beaten path and do right. Praying for them takes away the hate or resentment we have; because the simple truth is, sometimes it is hard to love an addict. It is so easy to pray though, and I have gotten so good at it. I've also gotten good at forgiving. It's not a weakness to forgive. Forgiveness, just like praying, makes us stronger. When we let go of past hurts and pains, we can celebrate a more resilient tomorrow. For some people, it is very difficult to forgive, because they wear that hurt and bury it deep down inside of them, so that it becomes a part of their identity.

" 'So and so' is just like that, because

she had a rough childhood, so it's ok."

"He is that way towards women,

because he comes from a broken home."

We are not our pasts, unless we continue to hold the shards of abuse close to our hearts and let them cut out every chance we have of being who God designed us to be. We have to learn to let it go.

David had his best soldier killed, just to hide the adulterous affair he committed with the soldier's wife that produced an offspring; that warrants forgiveness in the hearts of believers. Peter lost his faith, and that, too, warrants forgiveness by us believers. God forgave these men and now we all know the names David and Peter.

We think of these parables, and we relish in what they imply in our faith, but when there is a mention to forgive someone who has trespassed against us in an immoral way, we hesitate to forgive.

It's terrible to live with such a dual consciousness. We must choose to ALWAYS forgive, in the same manner that our Heavenly Father forgives. None of us are perfect, regardless if we are sober or drunken. We all fall short of the glory of God. Remember that when your alcoholic father forgets to pay the rent again, or when your addicted brother steals money from you. God forgives and so should you. That's all.

My name is Robert and I am an addict...I loved my children when I used drugs. It wasn't the right kind of love, but it was a love that I kept with me. I kept that love with me until I could love them the right way. Thank you, God. That's all.

(1Peter 1:15) But as He that called you is holy, so be ye holy in all manners of conversation.

RENEW, REEDUCATE, REFORM

In recovery, there are some changes that we have to make, which will disconnect us from our addictive thinking. See no evil, hear no evil, speak no evil, and, most importantly, seek no evil. It is hard for an addict to believe in God, because if we cannot taste it, see it or touch it, we don't want it. We need to smoke it, sniff it up, or drink it to believe in it, or we don't want it.

We have to stop reminiscing with our past and cease the rendezvous with drugs in our mind. Rid yourself of all thoughts about drugs and alcohol. No it won't be easy, but choose something you see everyday, like a bird or a tree and associate that with something positive like God's love. Every time I see a bird, I say a prayer or take a moment to talk with God. It keeps my thought from straying to the past and consumes me with positive thoughts that keep me centered. You won't believe how many birds I notice every single day, especially on the days that I need to be reminded that God is all around me. Stop reminiscing and find reminders of God's love. They are all around.

Renew, reeducate and reform your thinking process, and then the desire to use will disappear. Try it. Renew the way you view your family, reeducate yourself on the definition of love, and reform how you feel about yourself. You deserve to be happy. You deserve to be free from the shackles of addiction. Renew, reeducate and reform.

In recovery, we must admit that we must change. Put on the armor of a new man, dress yourself differently, create a different army around you. Do all you can to be the best you that you can possibly be. Renew, reeducate, and reform.

When all hope is gone, we still do not give up, because we realize that being lost is so close to being found.

My name is Robert Bauldwin and I am an addict. When I first stopped using, I was so angry with myself. I didn't know how to express myself. Therefore, the only thing that came out of me was foul language. However, as my anger began to dissipate, the more I began to like myself, and the easier it became to articulate how I felt without using any foul language. Being able to articulate has really helped me with my recovery. That ...and staying away from all things foul...that includes, foul words. That's all I have.

(Ephesians 4:29)
Let no corrupt communication proceed out of your mouth, but that which is good to the use of edifying, that it may minister grace unto the heavens.

(Phillippians 1:16) Being confident of this very thing that he, which hath begun a good work in you, will perform it until the end of the day of Jesus.

(1CORINTHIANS 3:16) *Know ye not that ye are the temple of God and that the spirit of God dwelleth in you.*

My name is Paris Bauldwin and I am the child of an addict. When I was in school, I used to get picked on a lot, because my clothes and shoes would often have holes in them. While the other girls' parents used to take them to salons to get their hair done, mine sometimes went days in the same ponytail, unbrushed.

I used to get bullied so badly, that I would sometimes sit in the bathroom during lunch, just so no one could find me to pick on me, because it was already enough that life seemed to be the most antagonizing bully. I would take the van to the shelter, and do my homework and cry myself to sleep, because life just didn't seem fair. It has been more than fair to me. I LOVE who and what I have become, not in spite of, but because of, my bullies, the real ones, and the intangible ones. It gets better...trust me. That's all.

(1Peter 3:10) For he that will love life and see good days, let him refrain his tongue from evil and his lips, they speak no guile.

My name is Robert and I am an addict. For some reason, when I was in the crack house, I had a strange feeling, and no it wasn't because I was high. I often had the odd feeling that someone would come and save me. I felt that someone would come, walk in the house, take me by the hand and walk me out of the door. Finally, that person came along; it was me. That's all.

Many of us, when we first came into A.A, we didn't think we would make it, but we did. Do not give up on your recovery. God is working on and through you. Let Him finish.

CHANGE GONNA COME

In A.A, we cannot say we have a higher power, but in our works, deny Him. After we leave the meeting, we cannot forget about the rededication moments, when we gave glory to God for life and sobriety. Continue to glorify Him in all you do and at all times. It's going to require some work on your part, but it's a necessary, welcomed change.

We have already acknowledged that we must change. The ways of our life we had grown accustomed to were destroying, not only our lives, but the lives of the people we loved. We must change in a different way in order to stay sober. Ephesians 4:22-23 tells us, "That ye put off concerning the former conversation the old man, which is corrupt according to the deceitful lusts; And be renewed in the spirit of your mind".

We must change our thought process in order to stay sober. We must make our families our number one priority, instead of getting high. We must learn that things of the past have occurred in order to improve our futures. We must program our minds to be more God like in all aspects of our life, and accept that we are new men and women in our sobriety.

(Ephesians 2:1-2) 1And you hath he quickened, who were dead in trespasses and sins; 2Wherein in time past ye walked according to the course of this world, according to the prince of the power of the air, the spirit that now worketh in the children of disobedience:

My name is Robert Bauldwin and I am an addict. In the A.A book, step nine says to make direct amends with people you have hurt, wherever possible, except if doing so would cause harm. I thank God when I awake and have an opportunity to right the wrongs that I have made.

All it takes is simply saying, "Forgive me." It is so simple. Do not let the opportunity to ask for forgiveness pass you by. Simplify your deliverance; say those two small words, "forgive me". Do not let the sun go down on an opportunity to say those words to someone you have hurt, because it may very well be your last sunset. That's all.

(Romans 13:13) Let us walk honestly, as in the day; not in rioting and drunkenness, not in chambering and wantonness, not in strife and envying.

When you first stop using drugs, don't you think that you are the Messiah. Don't go thinking that you are the one that will bring salvation to the crack house. Believe me, it won't work.

You see, if I understand where I used to be, I can understand where I need to be.

THE GOD IN ME

God told us that He would dwell in us, because we are the temple of God. You don't need to go to a building to find God; He lives in you. All you have to do is look inside of yourself. God will direct your steps.

When you feel alone and don't have the strength to maintain, know that God lives in you and will give you strength. Sometimes we are so down in our addiction, we think God is so far away. Well I am here to tell you, God is not far from you. He is nearer to you than you could ever imagine, because you are the temple and God lives in you. You don't have to go out and seek Him out. He is with you always.

Be wise and cautionary of what you allow inside of that temple. What you allow inside, directly affects God's living *situation*. IF you pollute your temple and put too much junk in it, of course it won't allow for God to freely. His flow will be obstructed by the drugs, alcohol and whatever else you choose to allow inside, making it a little difficult for you to feel His presence.

Often times we make our house look good on this outside, but inside it is filthy, polluted, and corrupt, however, He is always there. Just keep the place clean for Him. Jesus said in Luke 17:20-21 when he was demanded by the Pharisees about when the Kingdom of God would arrive, he answered

20 The Kingdom of God cometh not with observation. 21 Neither shall they say lo here or lo there, for behold the kingdom of God is within you. All you have to do is look within yourself.

(Luke 11:38-40) 38 And when
the Pharisee saw it, he
marveled that he had not first
washed before dinner. 39And
the Lord said unto him, Now do
ye Pharisees make clean the
outside of the cup and the
platter; but your inward part is
full of ravening and
wickedness. 40Ye fools, did
not he that made that which is
without make that which is
within also?

In recovery, make sure you clean the house, inside and out.

God forever stays with those who believe in Him.

My name is Paris and I am the child of an addict...My
father once asked me why I had forgiven him for all of the things we had to
endure at the hand of his addiction, and honestly, forgiveness wasn't really a
choice for me. I didn't choose to forgive my father for all of the terrible things we
had to endure growing up; hunger pains from going without food, our time in a
foster home, days with no electricity in the middle of the winter...forgiveness
was not really a choice for me. It just came natural.

In life, there will be things that we are privileged to choose to do and then
there will be things that we do on our own with no second thought. I call that
God. The way I see it, all of the bad things we endured, are also testimony to the
things that God rescued my family and me from.

Yes, we were hungry and homeless, but now I have a roof over my head and
food in my refrigerator. Yes, we went without, but I am on a path that promises
to bear fruits exceeding and abundantly. Yes, we were broken, but now we are
fixed. God saved us from so much.

Considering the events of my path, I should be broken and tattered,
possibly strung out somewhere denied the opportunity to dream, however, I am
not, and I am so thankful to God that He chose to save me. How could I ever
think about denying His presence inside of me...His presence that warrants
forgiveness to all those that trespass against me. The fragments of my life are
pretty jaded and not very beautiful to look at if you glance at them individually,
however, the beautiful masterpiece that sits here now, is more precious than a
Picasso, because I know it was destined for me to have to endure the trials, so

that I could find my triumph. God selected me, and put me on a path of righteousness. WE ALL HAVE A PURPOSE IN LIFE and GOD made me a promise. I have to do my part to recoup the fruits of my faithfulness; forgiveness is a part of that.

Understand that no pain lasts forever, unless you allow it to. You have the right to turn any tribulation into something beautiful, because sometimes God's blessings come in the form of burdens; and I know it is cliché, but diamonds are really formed by pressure. It is all in His beautiful design.

This fragmented tapestry of life can be brutal and brittle at times, but overall, once you take a step back, you see the beauty in all the changes, all the tears, all the heartbreak, complied together made you the brilliant you that you are today. God doesn't allow accidents to occur. I am thankful for what seemed like constant rainclouds in my past. The beautiful sunny days that are ahead, seem so much more radiant now than they ever could have if I hadn't experienced some torrential rain. That's all.

(Hebrew 13:15) Therefore, let us offer the sacrifice of praise to God continuously that is; the fruit of our lips giving thanks to His name.

STRONG WINDS

When you cease to surrender to the compulsive and rigorous activity of using drugs, and step back, and take time to realize the severity of the aftermath of the storm that had engulfed you, you realize there is a warrior inside of you. That warrior survived during a violent storm that impeded without any acknowledgment from you. You walked through this storm unharmed and unaffected because as the trees were violently tossed and homes drastically destroyed, you became so used to the chaos and accepted it as normal. Now that the warrior is aware of the danger of the storm and the conditions are acknowledged, you are determined to get out of the storm. Although it seems to be a daunting task, warrior, the spirit of grace, will give you strength.

Once the dissent begins, you must continuously remind yourself that greatness resides inside of you, because greater is He that is in you than he that is in the world. You must add faith to your grace, and virtue to your faith. Once you have done that you have to add knowledge to your virtue and patience to your knowledge; then patiently move to the end of the storm.

Now look out, through the eye of the storm, and see the serenity of a sober life...a sober life with Jesus. Be careful, for the eye of the storm. You have to continue through to make it to the end. The storm gets more violent as you pass through the eye and attempt to make it to the other side.

Strong winds accompanied by rain, snow, hail, make the trip more and more violent. The storm knows you are out of breath and wants you to give up and just give in to defeat, because the breakthrough is near. The storm is trying its hardest to detract you from Jesus, who is waiting on the other side. Although, a relapse seems more reasonable than continuing, just know all you have to do is reach out your arm and Jesus will pull you through the rest of the way. He was always beside you, and inside you giving you strength, even through the rising tides. If you let Him, he will pull you through the storms of life. Just let Him.

We find out what we are made of when our faith is tested.

My name is Robert and I am an addict... Today I have eight years, and I thank God, my wife, and my children and you all here, in these rooms of the A.A. Being around people that like me for who I am, allows me to quit being the great pretender.

I have had a lot of good times with my wife and my children. The most precious times are when I seem them smile or hear their voices on the phone. It brings tears to my eyes, when I think of them, and how much they mean to me. There are plenty of bad times I experience in my sober life, but the good times far outweigh the bad...they are the best. This is life, I guess. I never really knew it before, but this is life. That's all.

Romans 12:3 For I say, through the grace given unto me, to every man that is among you, not to think of himself more highly than he ought to think; but to think soberly, according as God hath dealt to every man the measure of faith.

And the very God of peace, sanctifies you wholly. (Thessalonians 5:23-24

Recovery means to change.

> (Galatians 4:9) But now after that ye have known God or rather are known of God, how turn ye again to the weak and beggarly elements. Whereunto ye desire again to be in bondage.

If you relapse go back in as soon as you can.

My name is Robert Bauldwin and I am an addict... I have 8 and ½ years of sobriety and today, I feel like one more...That's all.

I love you, daddy

When people relapse, it is not just our return to drugs; it is a departure from God. It is us walking away from God. Is it really worth it?

Become a man again. Stop using drugs and rule your home again. Be not drugged and drunk, but be filled with the spirit of God.

In A.A, it is good to share your story.

Sometimes silence is the best weapon when evil is present.

Be good to yourself in recovery.

Find recovery today.   *Love yourself*

MY NAME IS ROBERT BAULDWIN...Today I put God first in my life, and His son Jesus, even though now things are very hard. I have not worked in almost three years and my wife has been unable to find a job. We were recently in a terrible car accident that landed us both in the ICU, where it was detected that I have lung cancer.

We are at rock bottom and life isn't great, but we still give thanks to God because we have faith that everything will be okay. God is working through us where we are and even though we don't see how, we believe that all that we desire is already in route to us. Our faith will take us to better days. That's all.

After (words)

My father was an incredible man. He lost his battle with cancer last year, and I have to say, I miss him so incredibly much. His death came right on the heels of my God sister, Lashawna, who died in a terrible accident, celebrating her birthday. The fragility of life became so apparent in the 48 hours between the two deaths. Unbearable pain and sadness followed, as I tried to grasp why these lives were taken so soon; Lashawana was only 30 and my father 51. Healing came in relinquishing my desire to understand why, and accepting God's perfect will over everything.

Lashawna was one of the most beautiful people that ever graced the earth. Her smile and laughter was so contagious and her energy so absolutely captivating. I keep that with me everyday. She touched so many hearts, and will continue to do so through her beautiful daughter.

My father's wisdom and strength are my own now. I recall his faith in my own times of weakness. Jean, his wife, told me that my father used to pray so much and for so long, that there were times when she had no idea where he would be. One day in particular, my father was missing for nearly an entire day. Jean had gotten worried and called my uncles, and no one knew where he was. As the sun set, and worry continued to settle in, Jean got in bed to pray. Upon, doing so, she heard a voice in the closet. She opened the closet door and found my dad on his knees crying out to God. He had been in that closet, praying all day.

He had become my best friend. Whenever, I was having a bad day with school or life in general I called him, because he was so grounded in the word of God, that he always knew the right things to say. I am so thankful that God allowed me the opportunity to grow closer to him through writing this book. He would often call me and ask me how to spell a word, or read me a paragraph and ask me if it sounded alright. I took those moments for granted a bit when he was still around, but I cherish those memories now, as though they are rare gems.

Time has made missing them a little easier, but the months that followed their passings, were some of the hardest in my life. When you talk to someone almost every day, it becomes crippling when you can't hear their voice. My father's cancer had spread to his throat, as it advanced, so at times, I find it hard to even remember what his voice sounded like.

Some days are easy...some days are tough, like the days when I hear my friends pick up the phone to call their dads to tell them about boys or vent about car issues. I get sad sometimes when I think about how he will never be able to play with any of my children (when I am ready to have them) or walk me down the aisle (when I find my prince charming). But I am so thankful everyday because through writing this book, I got to tell, not only his story and aid him with fulfilling a life goal, but I got to share my own story, in a way that has helped me grow immensely.

The purpose of this book is to help, hopefully more, but at least one person; whether the addict or a family member or friend of an addict. Recently, talking with friends about the book, I learned that many of the people that are near and dear to my heart, have also been affected by a family member's addiction, we just never opened the dialogue about it. We are that much closer as friends because of what is reflected in us from our pasts. Begin the dialogue, talk about the wounds. It's good for the soul.

There are spelling errors and grammatical mistakes, but the purpose is to help spread love and understanding. God has you exactly where you are for a reason. Whether you are at a standstill, flying forward, or falling back, God has you reading this book, right now for a reason. Trust that your steps are purposed.

Take from it what you can about life and love and keep it with you as you piece together your own fragments. I love you. Be blessed.

Paris Bauldwin

Last Thoughts

My name is Robert Bauldwin and I am an addict...I have been asking all my brothers to write down my mom's last words to each of them. I was out of it emotionally, physically, and spiritually, when she passed away. In my addiction, I hated being around my mother's death, although in my addiction, death was something that was around me all the time.

I feel so ashamed that in my mother's final hours, I became a coward and I missed her good byes. Those kinds of goodbyes don't come back. I know that I must let go, but I carry that offense with me always. I will always remember her smile, though, and her courage to face death with victory. I can't wait to see her again.

I dedicate this book, and all my works to her, my children, and my beautiful wife. Take today to change your life. Don't continue to do things that you will have to regret or bare scars for later. Take control of your life, because you never know when it will be taken away. Love yourself...and continue your walk with God, even if you misstep, continue to walk with him. That's all.

You are not alone in your pain

You are not alone, and no one ever struggles in vain

For the Lord has great plans for your life

He has written for you to have sorrows, agonies, and strife

But He has also promised you abundance, greatness and light

Let HIS light shine through.

See HIM in all things that happen to you.

Hold your head high and go forth, fearless,

Write the next chapter according to all that you have witnessed.

You are not alone. You are not alone.

www.ingramcontent.com/pod-product-compliance
Lightning Source LLC
Chambersburg PA
CBHW032003040426
42448CB00006B/466